THE Dickens
DICTIONARY

An A-Z of England's Greatest Novelist

JOHN SUTHERLAND

ICON

Published in the UK in 2012 by
Icon Books Ltd, Omnibus Business Centre,
39–41 North Road, London N7 9DP
email: info@iconbooks.co.uk
www.iconbooks.co.uk

Sold in the UK, Europe, South Africa and Asia
by Faber & Faber Ltd, Bloomsbury House,
74–77 Great Russell Street,
London WC1B 3DA or their agents

Distributed in the UK, Europe, South Africa and Asia
by TBS Ltd, TBS Distribution Centre, Colchester Road,
Frating Green, Colchester CO7 7DW

Published in Australia in 2012
by Allen & Unwin Pty Ltd,
PO Box 8500, 83 Alexander Street,
Crows Nest, NSW 2065

ISBN: 978-184831-391-0

Typeset in Minion by Marie Doherty

Printed and bound in the UK by
CPI Group (UK) Ltd, Croydon, CR0 4YY

About the author

John Sutherland is the recently retired Lord Northcliffe Professor Emeritus at University College London: a title that one feels Dickens might have had some fun with. He has taught and published widely, particularly on Victorian fiction. His most recent relevant books are *The Longman Companion to Victorian Fiction* (Longman, 2009) and *Lives of the Novelists: A History of Fiction in 294 Lives* (Profile, 2011). He and Stephen Fender published *Love, Sex, Death and Words: Surprising Tales from a Year in Literature* with Icon Books in 2010.

In Memoriam
K.J. Fielding

Contents

Preface

2012 will be a year memorable for a British diamond jubilee, a British Olympic Games, and the commemoration of the country's greatest novelist. How best to approach Charles Dickens? There may be readers who, like the boa-constrictor and the goat, can swallow Dickens whole. I personally have known only three: Philip Collins (who taught me as an undergraduate), K.J. Fielding (who supervised my PhD) and Michael Slater (a colleague at the University of London).

I admire the work of these scholars and I have used it (gratefully). But it seems to me that there is another approach, and one that is more appropriate to that peculiarity of the Dickensian genius: its infinite variety and downright oddness. When I think of Dickens I do not see a literary monument, but an Old Curiosity Shop, stuffed with surprising things: what the Germans call a *Wunderkammer* – a chamber of wonders.

This book, taking as its starting point 100 words with a particular Dickensian flavour and relevance, is a tour round the curiosities, from the persistent smudged fingerprint picked up in the blacking factory in which Dickens suffered as a little boy to the nightmares he suffered from his unwise visit at feeding time to the snake-room of London Zoo.

One of the wonderful things about this wonderful author is that, like Shakespeare, there can never be any final 'explanations', or 'readings'. Merely an inexhaustible fund of entertainment or, as Sleary the circus master (see the first entry) would call it, 'amuthement'. The 'Great Entertainer' one Gradgrindian critic (F.R. Leavis) called him, intending belittlement. I see it as a term of the highest literary praise.

Dickens will sell more copies of his fiction in 2012 than he did in any year of his life and – I would bet – any year since his death. To pick up any of his novels, and turn any of the pages, is to understand why. He entertains. So, I hope, will what follows.

John Sutherland
January 2012

✍ Amuthement ❧

In *Hard Times* the lisping circus-owner Sleary repeats, like a parrot with Tourette's syndrome (an epidemic condition in Dickens's fiction), his rule of life: 'People mutht be amuthed.' Sleary, in terms of his narrative presence, is very much a peripheral figure, but on the subject of the human need for something other than pedagogic instruction he has full Dickensian authority.

Hard Times is what the Victorians called a 'Social Problem Novel', centred on the wholly unamusing Preston mill-workers' strike of 1854. Dickens locates Preston's social problem as originating in what Carlyle called 'cash nexus': the belief that the only bond between mill-owner and mill-hand was the money that passed between them. This hard-nosed hard-headedness (hard-heartedness?) Dickens associated with the Manchester school of economics – Utilitarianism.

Economists scorn Dickens's amateurish grasp of their dismal science. But where 'amuthement' was concerned he was expert. Utilitarianism, he felt, was anti-life. It did to human existence what maps do to landscape. It's exemplified in Bitzer's disintegrated definition of a horse (he's the prize-pupil in Thomas Gradgrind's school).

> Quadruped. Graminivorous. Forty teeth, namely twenty-four grinders, four eye-teeth, and twelve incisive. Sheds coat in the spring; in marshy countries, sheds hoofs, too. Hoofs hard, but requiring to be shod with iron. Age known by marks in mouth.

The 1850s, when Dickens serialised *Hard Times* in his weekly paper, *Household Words*, saw an explosion in the travelling circus. They specialised in clever canines and trick equestrianism –

Mr Gradgrind objects sternly to the circus.

the original horse and pony show. The big ones might even have elephants. Dickens alludes to the wondrous jumbo in his description of the great factory in Preston ('Coketown') 'where the piston of the steam-engine worked monotonously up and down, like the head of an elephant in a state of melancholy madness'. How, one shudderingly wonders, would Bitzer describe that quadruped?

Hard Times opens in a schoolroom with Gradgrind laying down his educational theory: 'Now, what I want is, Facts. Teach these boys and girls nothing but Facts. Facts alone are wanted in life.' To which Dickens responds: 'What about Fiction?'

A few months before the great strike, Manchester opened the country's first free public library. But what to put in it? The utilitarian authorities decreed Gradgrindish 'factuality'. No, insisted Dickens. Fiction should also feature prominently on those library shelves (he, too, was a trade-unionist of kinds: just like those millworkers). His plea was borne out by the first statistics (Manchester loved what Cissy Jupe calls 'stutterings'). The most popular book borrowed from the library was *The Arabian Nights*. Dickens refers to it frequently in his novel.

Point proved by Sinbad the Sailor and Jumbo the Pachyderm. People mutht be amuthed. But it would, alas, be some years before the Manchester Public Library stocked the work of that most amusing of writers, Boz.

✎ Architectooralooral ✍

Every reader of *Great Expectations* laughs at the above malapropism. Joe Gargery, the blacksmith with muscles of iron and a heart of gold, has come up to London – his first visit, we apprehend. He calls on Pip, now well on the way to becoming an arrant snob. 'Have you seen anything of London, yet?' asks Pip's housemate, Herbert. 'Why, yes, Sir', replies Joe,

Hungerford Stairs, where the young Dickens suffered.

'me and Wopsle went off straight to look at the Blacking Ware'us. But we didn't find that it come up to its likeness in the red bills at the shop doors; which I meantersay,' added Joe, in an explanatory manner, 'as it is there drawd too architectooralooral.'

This is not Warren's boot-blacking factory by Hungerford Stairs where the twelve-year-old Charles was put to work while his father was in debtors' prison, but the imposing Day and Martin establishment at 97 High Holborn. It was not the first sight a tourist on his first trip to London – even one as ingenuous as Joe Gargery – would seek out. The coded reference is clear enough. *Great Expectations* is an autobiographical novel and this is a sliver of raw autobiography.

During his lifetime Dickens told only his designated biographer, John Forster, about his blacking factory ordeal as a child. But it pleased him to slip in sly references in his fiction. In *Nicholas*

Nickleby there is a passing reference to a 'sickly bedridden hump-backed boy', whose only pleasure is 'some hyacinths blossoming in old blacking bottles'. The 'Warren' figures centrally in *Barnaby Rudge*. Most direct is the description of the Grinby and Quinion factory in his other autobiographical novel, *David Copperfield*:

> It was a crazy old house with a wharf of its own, abutting on the water when the tide was in, and on the mud when the tide was out, and literally overrun with rats. Its panelled rooms, discoloured with the dirt and smoke of a hundred years, I dare say; its decaying floors and staircase; the squeaking and scuffling of the old grey rats down in the cellars; and the dirt and rottenness of the place; are things, not of many years ago, in my mind, but of the present instant. They are all before me, just as they were in the evil hour when I went among them for the first time, with my trembling hand in Mr Quinion's.

Dickens also never forgot. Warren's blacking is no longer available in the shops, but for those who look carefully there is a trembling black fingerprint smudging every page he wrote.

෨ Art ෧

Dickens lived through a revolutionary period of art in Britain and Europe. Across the Channel, Impressionism re-imagined the visible world. The American artist, Whistler, threw his paint pot in the face of the British public – and went to court against art critic John Ruskin to justify the act. Ruskin himself fathered the most revolutionary home-grown movement, the Pre-Raphaelite Brotherhood.

Dickens was – viewed from one angle – an artistic impresario. Ever since ousting the luckless Robert Seymour from the *Pickwick Papers* (and turning down a hopeful young W.M. Thackeray as not a good enough draughtsman) he instructed a series of leading artists exactly how they should illustrate the Dickens texts. All his monthly series had two full-page etchings on steel and an illustrated wrapper. His later serials featured woodcuts and new lithographic technologies.

The roll call of artists who worked for (not with) Dickens is impressive: George Cruikshank, Hablot Knight Browne, Luke Fildes, George Cattermole, Daniel Maclise, Clarkson Stanfield, Richard Doyle, Samuel Williams, Samuel Palmer.

Dickens's initial preference was for the light-fingered cartoon/sketch, as practised by Cruikshank. In his later career he favoured 'dark plates' – static and realistic. Luke Fildes's 'veritable photographs' (as Dickens called them) for *Edwin Drood* represent the endpoint of the journey from the Cruikshankery of *Oliver Twist*.

Luke Fildes, from *The Mystery of Edwin Drood*, 1870.

Dickens, scholars have argued, actually and literally *saw* the world differently at the end of his life. Photography had made a new reality.

Dickens's dictates to his artists (none of whom were munificently paid) were underpinned by conventional taste verging on prejudice. He wrote nothing more alarmingly prejudiced, critically, than his hysterical assault on John Millais' early Pre-Raphaelite masterpiece, 'Christ in the House of his Parents', as it was exhibited in the Royal Academy in summer 1850:

> You behold the interior of a carpenter's shop. In the foreground of that carpenter's shop is a hideous, wry-necked, blubbering, red-headed boy, in a bed-gown, who appears to have received a poke in the hand, from the stick of another boy with whom he has been playing in an adjacent gutter, and to be holding it up for the contemplation of a kneeling woman, so horrible in her ugliness, that (supposing it were possible for any human creature to exist for a moment with that dislocated throat) she would stand out from the rest of the company as a Monster, in the vilest cabaret in France, or the lowest ginshop in England.

It's a grotesque outbreak of Podsnappery in a man whose judgement, in virtually everything of any importance, was normally so sound. When it came to art, Dickens was that awful English thing – 'the man who knew what he liked'.

ᴄᴏ **Baby Farming** ᴏᴄ

Few great writers have been less interested in tilling the soil than Dickens. There was, however, one kind of farming that excited his interest – baby farming. It seems on the face of it a Swiftian fantasy of the *Modest Proposal* kind. But baby-farming was big business in the early 1840s.

During the cholera epidemic of 1849 (*see* 'Blue Death') there was death everywhere in London, but on total extinction level at the Drouet Establishment for Pauper Children in Tooting. The institution had been set up in 1825, as a dump for the metropolis' unowned offspring.

By law they had to be looked after by the London authorities until they were fourteen – when the workhouse opened its uncharitable doors to them unless, like Oliver Twist, they could be farmed out again as pseudo-apprentices (many of the girls went straight into prostitution). Education, or any preparation for life, in the farm was virtually non-existent.

There were some 1,400 inmates at Drouet's establishment in 1849 yielding four shillings and sixpence per head, per week, from public funds. They were crammed into accommodation worse than the black hole of Calcutta. Almost 200 died of cholera, over the half the children were infected.

A first inspection whitewashed Peter Drouet, the owner. It was bad air ('atmospheric poison') from London that was at fault. A second inspection, as the death rate soared, was highly critical. If there was indeed 'atmospheric poison' it was from the luckless children's excrement, which made the inspectors retch. There was not a single case of cholera in Tooting (then green-field countryside), outside Drouet's pest hole.

Dickens fired off four articles in his paper, *Household Words*. They burned with sarcastic indignation against 'the Paradise in Tooting'. Following a series of damning inquests, Peter Drouet was brought to trial. A skilful defence team got him acquitted. The cholera was an act of God, the court determined.

One good thing came out of the trial. As Dickens concluded in his fourth article:

> He [Drouet] was 'affected to tears' as he left the dock. It might be gratitude for his escape, or it might be grief that his occupation was put an end to. For no one doubts that the child-farming system is effectually broken up by this trial. And every one must rejoice that a trade which derived its profits from the deliberate torture and neglect of a class the most innocent on earth, as well as the most wretched and defenceless, can never on any pretence be resumed.

Dickens, baby-saver, can take some credit for that.

⍟ Back-Stories ⍟

With some principal characters in Dickens's fiction we know the back-stories. With others, tantalisingly, we don't. It's not a small thing. In some novels – *Bleak House* notably – back-stories (those of Esther, Rouncewell, Lady Dedlock, Nemo) rise gradually to the surface and *are* the novel. What lies untold in the lives of other characters will baffle even readers of the most speculative cast of mind.

Great Expectations opens with Pip contemplating a family hecatomb. The gravestones of his mother, father, and five siblings record nothing but the fact of death. What wiped out the Pirrips? What did Pip's father do for a living? Was his mother a gentle lady – or a shrew who lives on, shrewishly, in her daughter Mrs Joe?

There are further mysteries in the marriage of Mr and Mrs Joe. Why are she and Joe Gargery childless? It is not, as later events prove, sterility on his part: he and Biddy procreate soon enough.

We can guess (without the slightest supporting evidence other than her extraordinary bitterness and those frightening pins in her apron) that she allows no conjugal liberties with her body. Why is she so angry at the world and her husband? It's the more curious since she's married to one of the nicest men ever to draw breath in Dickens's fiction. Was she, like Miss Havisham (no mystery about that back-story) jilted at the altar?

Joe's back-story we do know. He recounts it to Pip in some detail in Chapter 7. His brutal, drunken father 'hammered' him and his mother, 'most onmerciful'. Nonetheless, Joe (blindly) insists that his father 'was good in his hart'. Why did Joe – with this background – not grow up a drunken thug like his father? As the twig is bent, so the tree is bent. That, usually, is the law of Dickens's universe. Joe, mysteriously, grows straight.

Magwitch recounts a very similar back-story to Joe's, in Chapter 42, explaining to Pip how he was 'hardened' by childhood abuse into a criminal and a murderer. Doubtless Bill Sikes, the unspeakable brute in *Oliver Twist*, could have told the same tale. How has Joe contrived to preserve his softness?

There's no clear answer. Dickens, we deduce, loved contraries as much as William Blake. He could adhere – in the case of Magwitch – to the view that, as William Godwin put it, 'circumstances create crime'. He could simultaneously adhere to the quite opposite view that 'good harts' can rise above any circumstance. But not, alas, very often. There are more Sikeses than Joe Gargerys in Dickens's world.

∞ Bastards ∞

Children born out of wedlock are as common as fleas in Dickens's dramatis personae (16,000 characters make up the population of the Dickens world, it's reckoned). Fagin's little pickers and stealers are almost certainly illegitimate. At least half the sad enrolment of Dotheboys Hall in *Nicholas Nickleby*, one can plausibly assume, are legally unowned by any parent.

Three of Dickens's novels, *Oliver Twist*, *Barnaby Rudge* and *Bleak House*, hinge on bastardy. In the hierarchy of unlucky children the illegitimate rank lower than orphans (like Pip) but higher than street urchins (like Jo in *Bleak House*). Bastards, in Dickens's fictional universe, invariably discover their mysterious parentage – as, in melodramatic circumstances, do Oliver, Esther Summerson, Estella, and Hugh the Ostler.

Until the 1960s British law and society were cruelly prejudiced towards children born out of wedlock. They had no inheritance rights – not even to their father's name (if known). The bastard carried an indelible stigma through life. What had they done to deserve it? They were born.

Dickens uses his bastardy McGuffin in different ways. Hugh in *Barnaby Rudge* is more brutal even than the horses whose droppings he shovels. He places himself at the head of the Gordon riots – wielding murderous axe and torch – only to discover, late in the day, that he is the offspring of Sir John Chester. As the rope goes round his own neck, Hugh curses 'that man who in his conscience owns me for his son'.

Blue blood, Dickens argues, does not – as English society fools itself – make for 'good breeding'. *Oliver Twist* makes a quite opposite point. 'The old story', sighs the workhouse attendant looking down at the ringless hand of the hero's mother. But, bastard that he may be, Oliver has a gentility gene. Surely a parish boy brought up among the Mudfog riff-raff would say 'Gissamore!' not 'Please, sir, I want some more'. By their accent may ye know them.

Ellen Ternan, 'the invisible woman'.

Esther in *Bleak House* makes a third point. Her 'godmother' (i.e. aunt – disinclined to own the relationship) tells her, by way of birthday present: 'Your mother, Esther, is your disgrace, and you were hers.' Nonetheless, as the novel progresses, no heroine in Dickens's fiction reveals herself to be morally less disgraceful than Esther, Mr Jarndyce's 'Dame Durden'. Goodness is goodness – whatever is missing in the register of births, marriages, and deaths.

Two things are odd. Only once does the b-word itself intrude onto Dickens's printed page, when the obnoxious Monks hurls the

imprecation at his hated half-brother, Oliver Twist. The other oddity is that bastardy, as a Dickensian plot device, disappears from his
pages around 1860.

Two explanations are offered. Most likely is that Dickens himself had a 'love child' (as he would not have called it) by Ellen
Ternan, his mistress. The wilder speculation is that having separated from Mrs Dickens, mother of his ten legitimate children, he
had an incestuously engendered child by his sister-in-law Georgina
(in the imbroglio of the separation there were some ugly medical
investigations to certify her virginity). A ring once belonging to a
claimant of the 'Dickens – bar sinister' title was sold at auction in
January 2009 for £9,000.

◡◠ Bedding ◠◡

The bed is an important article in the Dickens world. The greater
part of *A Christmas Carol*, for example, happens while Scrooge is
lying in bed. No deathbeds are more famous than those of Little
Nell and Paul Dombey.

Oliver Twist's re-ascent to the station in life to which he belongs
is marked by the beds he lies in. He is born on a 'workus' bed – a
crude pallet, we assume, as his little body is wrenched, heartlessly,
from the body of his dying mother. At Sowerberry's, the under-
taker, his bed is a straw mattress under the counter, alongside the
coffins. In Fagin's den he occupies one of the hessian sacks (sleeping bags of a kind) alongside his fellow thieves.

Finally, he rests on respectable linen after he is taken in by
Brownlow. This, we apprehend, is where he should end up. So too
should Fagin end up as in the Cruikshank illustration, sitting on
his prison bunk: no sleep for the wicked on that punitive palliasse.

No rest for Fagin.

Dickens himself had idiosyncratic bed-rituals, designed to produce serene slumber. When travelling, he carried a pocket compass with him. This was for night-time use. He would insist that his bed for the night be placed so that the headboard faced due north. When he composed himself for sleep, Dickens would situate himself centrally within the bed by extending his arms full out, in a kind of crucifixion pose, so as to establish absolute equidistance from the two edges.

He was as particular about his final resting place as he was in life. He instructed in his will: 'that my name be inscribed in plain English letters on my tomb. I rest my claims to the remembrance of my country upon my published works.'

Initially he was to be entombed at Rochester Cathedral (emblematised in the frontispiece to *Edwin Drood*). Public opinion, mobilised by *The Times*, insisted instead that Poets' Corner in Westminster Abbey should be his final resting place. On 14 June he was interred in an empty cathedral (only an apostolic dozen mourners were admitted) under the plainest of headstones, which he had decreed.

In 1935 an attempt to have his body exhumed and returned to Rochester, where the town felt it belonged, was rejected. I have recently been to examine the Westminster memorial. His head, I am sad to say, does not, by my compass, point north. RIP, nonetheless, and sucks to Rochester.

✎ Blade or Rope? ✐

Dickens was always curious about the best way to kill people. People, that is, who deserved to be killed. He gave the question considerable thought in the 1840s. The central issue, as he put it in a newspaper article of 1845, was that

> Society [has] arrived at that state, in which it spares bodily torture to the worst criminals: and [has] agreed, if criminals be put to Death at all, to kill them in the speediest way.

But what was the 'speediest way'? He pondered the question during his family trip to Italy in the mid-1840s when, in Rome, he witnessed a beheading. The victim richly deserved the axe. He had waylaid a countess on pilgrimage, robbed her, before beating her to death with her own pilgrim's staff.

Dickens observed the execution with a novelist's eye, a tourist's curiosity, an Englishman abroad's prejudices, and a penal reformer's interest. The condemned man was brought to the platform

> bare-footed; his hands bound; and with the collar and neck of his shirt cut away, almost to the shoulder. A young man – six-and-twenty – vigorously made, and well-shaped. Face pale; small dark moustache; and dark brown hair ... He immediately kneeled down, below the knife. His neck fitting into a hole, made for the purpose, in a cross plank, was shut down, by another plank above; exactly like the pillory. Immediately below him was a leathern bag. And into it his head rolled instantly.
>
> The executioner was holding it by the hair, and walking with it round the scaffold, showing it to the people, before one quite knew that the knife had fallen heavily, and with a rattling sound.

Whatever else, those Italians did their bloody work with enviable 'speed'. But importing their efficient blade into England was tricky. It was not English. And beheading was, traditionally, a privilege of aristocracy. It went against the populist grain to honour every criminal Tom, Dick and Harry with it. Whatever next? Silken hang ropes?

But how to get that necessary 'speed'? Fagin, for example, would have dangled and strangled, dancing on the end of the rope for up to twenty minutes while the spectators laughed uproariously at his hilarious death-jig. No wonder Oliver faints.

British penology was as worried as Dickens and experimented with a variety of 'drops' and 'knots' to introduce the necessary 'humanity' (i.e. speed) with the traditional rope and gallows. By the time John Jasper (as we assume Dickens planned) meets his end in the unfinished *Edwin Drood*, there were no more public hangings. He would have had a 'short drop' of some seven feet, calculated by his body weight, and the side knot would have 'speedily' snapped his neck. Problems solved.

Italy solved it a different way by abolishing capital punishment in the 1860s. Mussolini brought it back.

✆ **Blind Spots** ✆

There are black holes in Dickens's fiction that suck in speculation and emit no light. They are just there. He is, for example, the pre-eminent Victorian novelist who came to fame at almost the same moment that the young queen came to her throne. But can one find a single reference to Victoria in his Victorian fiction? Or to her 25th jubilee in *Bleak House* (compare, for example, with *In the Year of Jubilee* by Dickens's disciple, George Gissing, commemorating the golden anniversary in 1887)? Kings and queens – even French kings and queens, in *A Tale of Two Cities* – are notable by their absence. Is the vacant space republicanism? Or a blind spot?

Dombey and Son came out at precisely the same period that the Irish potato famine was ravaging and depopulating that country. Dickens was immensely popular in Ireland. He had a distinguished disciple (some would say rival) in Charles Lever, the 'Hibernian Boz'. But, for all the tears drawn for the destitute Jo the Sweeper in *Bleak House*, there is no glance across the Irish Sea at a calamity so horrific that it has been laid at England's door as colonial genocide. Indifference? Or a blind spot?

It's not a consistent blinkering. Dickens was very open-eyed about the Preston mill-workers' strike in *Hard Times*. He even made a trip to Coketown (as he calls it) to get eye-witness evidence. No blind spot in that novel. Similarly in *Little Dorrit* (specifically Chapter 10, on the Circumlocution Office) Dickens is wholly in tune with current anger at the bungling incompetence with which Whitehall had managed the Crimean War. No blind spot on that burning issue.

Opium figures frequently in Dickens's fiction and forms the magnificent opening, in a drug den, of *Edwin Drood*. But Dickens, who was in full fictional flow in the late 1840s, makes no reference to the iniquitous Opium Wars, which enforced collective drug addiction on the whole Chinese people – in the interest of boosting the East India Company's export revenues.

John Jasper wakes in the opium den.

Examples could be multiplied. Suffice it to say, you will find riches in Dickens's fiction but don't look for a comprehensive image of Victorian England in the work of the leading Victorian novelist. Try the *Illustrated London News* and *The Times* instead.

✑ Bloomerism ✑

The term alludes to one of the early stirrings of what we know as feminism. It centred on 'rational dress'. Why, in a so-called century of 'reform', were women imprisoned in crinolines, burdened with bustles, forced to pad their hair with chignons? Why not go the whole hog and manacle them, like Magwitch en route to Australia?

Why, to focus on one definitive garment, could ladies not wear rational trousers – 'bloomers' – the better to ride that exciting new invention, the bicycle, or the horse (throw away that side-saddle). Or, at least, wear clothing that would allow them more 'conveniently' to relieve their bladders outside the home? The first *chalets de convenance* for London ladies were in the Oxford Street department stores: there was a good commercial reason for keeping well-dressed customers in the store. It was not until late in the century that the Ladies' Sanitary Association (formed in 1857) had any success in establishing metropolitan female 'conveniences' for all.

The term 'bloomer' originates in 1850s America. It was inspired by Amelia Bloomer, the evangelist of what we now call the 'pant suit'. There are no trousered harridans in Dickens: nor any out-and-out feminists like Trollope's Baroness Banman, with her slogan 'ze manifest inferiority of ze tyrant sex'.

However in advance of his time elsewhere, Dickens was no friend to reform in this particular area. And he got a few hits in for the male sex, notably in *Bleak House*. Two women, Mrs Jellyby and

Mrs Pardiggle, both extraneous to the plot, illustrate his antipathy for what another anti-feminist called 'the shrieking sisterhood'.

American feminism was born in the abolition movements, in Boston. One sees something dangerously similar in Mrs Jellyby's 'telescopic philanthropy'. When the Borrioboola-Gha mission goes bad (the king having sold all his subjects into slavery to buy rum) we are told that Mrs J. has 'taken up with the rights of women to sit in Parliament'.

A more virulent stream of Dickensian satire is directed against Mrs Pardiggle. 'She was a formidable style of lady, with spectacles, a prominent nose, and a loud voice, who had the effect of wanting a great deal of room.' The lady's main offence is not merely that she has a protuberant nose, but the fact that she pokes it into the man's world. She does not know her place. 'I am a Visiting lady', she boasts:

> I am a Reading lady, I am a Distributing lady; I am on the local Linen Box Committee and many general committees; and my canvassing alone is very extensive – perhaps no one's more so.

Such women are dangerous – they must be laughed away. Dickens, alas, did not live long enough to discover how hard that would be.

∞ Blue Death ∞

Dickens's and Thackeray's major fiction of the late 1840s and 1850s – when, as the author of *Vanity Fair* put it, the two of them were 'fighting it out at the top of the tree' – was conducted against the backdrop of a raging epidemic. 52,000 Londoners died of cholera over the years 1848–49. More, that is, than British soldiers

King Cholera.

died four years later in the Crimea. The epidemic was the biggest such event since the plague year Defoe had immortalised.

Cholera appeared from nowhere in India in 1817. It was duly called the 'Indian' or 'Asiatic' cholera and – most graphically – the 'Blue Death'. Death was agonising and the victim's skin became alarmingly discoloured.

The first epidemic in England was in 1831–32. Dickens, like most of his contemporaries, knew exactly what caused cholera: 'miasma'. The miasmic thesis is graphically enunciated in his descriptions of the slum dwelling 'Tom-All-Alone's', in Chapter 46 of *Bleak House* (first published when the third epidemic wave was at its height):

> Even the winds are his messengers, and they serve him in these hours of darkness. There is not a drop of Tom's corrupted blood but propagates infection and contagion somewhere … There is not an atom of Tom's slime, not a cubic inch of any pestilential

gas in which he lives, not one obscenity or degradation about
him, not an ignorance, not a wickedness, not a brutality of his
committing, but shall work its retribution, through every order
of society, up to the proudest of the proud, and to the highest
of the high.

Thackeray was one of those stricken in the 1848–49 epidemic. His
novel in progress, *Pendennis*, was suspended as its author hovered
between life and death over the summer months while his fellow
citizens died in their tens of thousands. He was saved from their
fate, as he firmly believed, by Dickens dispatching his personal
physician, John Elliotson, to treat him. The volume edition of
Pendennis is dedicated to the doctor.

Thackeray too was a miasmatist. Both he and Dickens were
plumb wrong. A brilliant young doctor, John Snow, deduced that
the culprit was London's polluted water. He proved it by reference
to one pump in Broad Street, Soho (drawing added flavour, it later
emerged, from a neighbouring cess pit). Snow had the pump handle removed on 7 September 1853 and the infection waned. That
same month *Bleak House*, which Dickens had first considered calling 'Tom-All-Alone's', came to the end of its monthly run.

The pump, less handle, remains as a monument to Snow, as
does the John Snow pub a few yards away. Snow would have slaked
his thirst in neither: he was temperance.

✎ Blue Plaques ✐

Blue Plaques commemorate houses where notable Londoners
have lived. Dickens has left more blue china in his wake than most
such notables.

'Nomadic' barely describes his childhood. He was born in Mile End Terrace, in Portsmouth. A finer house than most that followed it boasted two bedrooms and an outside privy at the bottom of the garden – rarely unoccupied, one surmises. At this period such remote sanitary arrangements were much to be preferred, for health reasons, over the inside sand-cabinet. Young Charles would never use that outside convenience. Before he was two, the family moved on to a nearby lodging house before flitting on yet again. After some months the Dickens caravan, now seven strong, moved on to London to spend two years in Norfolk Street, by Tottenham Court Road.

The next hiccup in John Dickens's erratic clerical employment moved them on to Sheerness, then to Rochester in Kent where the now six-year-old Charles could say, with Pip, that he gained his first impression 'of the identity of things'. One of the first of those things would have been packing cases.

The family made one more stop before, a year later, John Dickens returned to work in London. Charles was now ten years old. In London, the Dickenses took up residence in Camden Town at 16 Bayham Street. It was then, as now, busy by day and wild by night. This tiny house was home to eight Dickenses (parents, five children, an unlucky relative, and a maid of all work). Momentarily they took possession of a grander house, nearer the centre of town in Gower Street, before the sky fell down on John.

Unpaid bills led to Charles, the oldest son (although at twelve years hardly 'old') being put to work in Warren's blacking factory. The rest of the family were packed off to the Marshalsea debtors' prison. Charles was billeted with friends north and south of the river.

On John's release, the Dickenses moved to Somers Town, near where Euston station now stands. It is ripped into non-existence,

16 Bayham Street.

as Staggs's Gardens, in *Dombey and Son*. Dickens had no love for the place. The family remained there for three years until Charles could no longer be supported at school and was set free to make his way in the world.

What effect did this extraordinary motility (ten homes in as many years) have on him? His education was imperfect. His personal psychology was deformed. He would always be rootless by nature and choice. Gad's Hill near Rochester, his final residence, incredibly, was the only house he ever owned. He could never be still. Any blue plaque had to be very fast to catch up with Boz.

The first of them went up in 1903.

❧ Bohemians ❧

Thackeray's closest male friends were drawn from his public-school days (Charterhouse), his university days (Cambridge – Trinity College), and the clubs (the Garrick, Athenaeum, Reform) in which he loved to spend his late-career days. George Eliot had her blue-stocking salons.

Dickens's entourage, by contrast, was dominated by what were called 'bohemians' – fast, loose, and dangerous fellows. The brightest, most talented, and most bohemian star among them was young (b. 1824) Wilkie Collins. He it was who took the secondary character in *Bleak House*, Inspector Bucket, and with *The Moonstone* created what T.S. Eliot (no less) would call the first and greatest detective novel ever written.

Collins it was who took Dickens's high-impact style and shaped it into a whole new genre – the sensation novel – with *The Woman in White*. A proud, if occasionally censorious patron/father figure, Dickens brought Wilkie on, publishing his pioneer works as serials in his weekly papers.

Wilkie's personal life was, to use the preferred Victorian term, 'irregular'. He was an opium addict (his eyes, said one observer, resembled 'bags of blood' after a heavy dose). He was afflicted with what was vaguely called 'gout' and may well have been syphilitic. He lived, simultaneously, with two women. And he was Dickens's bosom companion on 'jaunts' to Paris. They were not, one may assume, spent in the Louvre.

Another luminary in among the sub-Dickensian bohemians was George Augustus Sala (b. 1828). The illegitimate son of an opera singer, Sala was a first-rate journalist and second-rate novelist. A friend of Swinburne – whose taste for flagellation he shared – he was the co-author of a classic of Victorian pornography,

The Mysteries of Verbena House: Or Miss Bellasis Birched for Thieving. In 1867 Sala successfully sued a fellow journalist who described him as 'often drunk, always in debt, sometimes in prison, and totally disreputable'. Truth is no defence in English libel law.

A third and still younger member of the crew was Edmund Yates (b. 1831). A gifted and fluent journalist, editor, novelist and (like Dickens) a very popular platform performer, Yates was profligate and reckless. He spent seven weeks in prison for libel in 1885 and died shortly after of a heart attack in the Savoy. He was at the centre of the most serious spat between Dickens and Thackeray in 1856 when the latter had Yates expelled from the Garrick Club for conduct unbecoming a gentleman (with the implication, what did one expect from one of Dickens's set?). Relations between the two great novelists never quite mended.

Dickens entrusted the writing of his biography to his least bohemian friend John Forster. In that biography Wilkie Collins gets all of fifteen words.

✆ Book Reading ✆

There are two occasions in *Great Expectations* when Magwitch erupts, terrifyingly, into Pip's life. The first is at the churchyard in the marshes, in the opening chapter, where most of the hero's family are lying.

> 'Hold your noise!' cried a terrible voice, as a man started up from among the graves at the side of the church porch. 'Keep still, you little devil, or I'll cut your throat!'

The second occasion, fifteen years later, is in Chapter 39. Pip, now a swell young man about town, is living in lodgings in the Temple, with Herbert Pocket. He hears nearby St Paul's strike eleven and – at the same ominous hour – there is a sound on the stair outside.
Enter 'a man':

> Moving the lamp as the man moved, I made out that he was sub-stantially dressed, but roughly; like a voyager by sea. That he had long iron-gray hair. That his age was about sixty. That he was a muscular man, strong on his legs, and that he was browned and hardened by exposure to weather. As he ascended the last stair or two, and the light of my lamp included us both, I saw, with a stupid kind of amazement, that he was holding out both his hands to me.

Stupidity soon turns to horror.

These are two of the most memorable moments in the novel. But what is Pip doing, on both occasions, when Magwitch bursts into his life? He is reading. In the graveyard he is attempting to decipher the inscriptions on the gravestones – his first inquiry into the meaning of life and death. In the second scene he has been reading self-improvingly – a habit he strenuously kept up, he informs us, even at the height of his metropolitan dissipations. It's with his 'reading lamp' that Pip throws enough illumination on his visitor's face to recognise who (horror!) it is.

It's a small detail, but a telling detail. It was another novel-ist, Gorki, who said, 'books are my university'. Dickens concurs, and embeds the point centrally in his two great autobiographical novels (*David Copperfield*, of course, is the other). His British Museum reader's ticket was his passport to higher education.

Among the many memorials Dickens left (including his stark tablet in Westminster Abbey) not the least creditable is the Sotheran's Sales Catalogue of his books, sold shortly after his death. It is witness to a heroic autodidact.

To continue the quiz – what is the last thing Pip does with Magwitch as he lies dying in prison? He reads with him.

✺ Bookshop or Bookstall? ✺

There is a charming illustration to *Oliver Twist* by Cruikshank showing Mr Brownlow 'browsing'. The word, one recalls, refers specifically to cattle munching contentedly in their meadows.

It's a bookseller somewhere around Paternoster Row, we assume. Mr Brownlow is examining a volume in 'quires' (it has no binding – purchasers supplied that to their own taste). Title pages and sample illustrations are pinned up, like washing on a rope, as display ads. One can see the same ruminative pre-purchase practice in any high street bookshop today.

The action of *Oliver Twist* is set pretty much when the serial was published: the mid-1830s. And this, of course, was how the novel itself would have been offered to the reading world. That world was about to change: explosively.

By the 1850s W.H. Smith's had established their monopoly on the country's principal termini and stations. Their main item of sale was newspapers. Placards outside shouted out what the headlines were. Smith's also retailed books that the train passengers might 'read as they ran'. No one would 'browse' in such outlets. They would snatch, pay, and rush off to whatever platform.

The new tempo of life changed the book product: garishly covered 'yellowbacks' at low prices (around half a crown) dominated, along with serial-carrying magazines. Smith's, after the 1850s, had a circulating library. You could pick a volume up at your starting point and drop it off at your destination, having whisked through the pages as your train sped at anything up to an amazing 60mph. Everything was faster. Including books.

The bookstall in *Oliver Twist*.

∽ **Boz** ∾

In 1827 a late child was born to the Dickens family. He was grandly christened 'Augustus'. Charles, now fifteen, nicknamed the little stranger 'Moses' after the teenager in Oliver Goldsmith's *The Vicar of Wakefield*, who is sent off to sell the family horse at the local fair and returns not with the cash but 'a gross of green spectacles'. 'Moses' was nasalised into 'Boses', then shortened to 'Boz' (it should therefore, some Dickensians claim, be pronounced 'Boze'). The other noteworthy feature is that Moses became Boses/Boz because of Charles's perennial head colds. He was a martyr to his blocked nose. The mangled 'Boz' subsequently seems to have been turned back, mockingly, on Charles himself.

Augustus came at a low point in the Dickens family fortunes. John Dickens had been released from the Marshalsea debtors' prison (and Charles from his labour in Warren's blacking factory) a couple of years earlier. But in 1827 the family were destitute again and were evicted from their home. Charles was removed from school – with lifelong damage to his education. The last thing the Dickens tribe needed was another mouth to feed. The biblical Moses, one recalls, is thrown into the river. It was also a favoured means of birth control among the criminal classes in London.

It's not surprising that the Dickens family should have cleaved to the optimisms of Goldsmith's tale, with its promise that the Lord will provide for the respectably destitute. He did not, alas, provide for John Dickens.

Charles told his biographer John Forster that he adopted his brother's nickname as the sobriquet for his first ventures into print because '"Boz" was a very familiar household word to me, long before I was an author'. Comic pseudonymy (e.g. Thackeray's

The young Dickens, alias 'Boz'.

'Fitz-Boodle') was the usual way of creating a running byline in the anonymous columns of the press. Late in life, Dickens would do it again with his 'Uncommercial Traveller' pieces in the anonymous pages of *All the Year Round*.

Dickens dropped the Boz pseudonym after *Nicholas Nickleby* because it was too easily plagiarised ('Bos', 'Buzz' etc.) and legally unprotectable – there being no trademark regulation at the time. His title pages thereafter used his proper name. The echoic 'Phiz' was, however, retained by his illustrator, Hablot K. Browne, throughout his career. He in turn was plagued by an artist called 'Quiz'.

After a disastrous marriage and humiliating handouts from his brother, Augustus Dickens decamped to America where he went to the dogs. Charles declined to read his begging letters, saying in 1859: 'I have no hope of him.' The original Boz died wretchedly a few years later, aged 39.

ᨀ Busted Boiler ᨏ

Dickens feared, before he was even 30 years old, that he was in danger of 'busting the boiler'. The image was that of a runaway train going faster and faster, until the machine could take no more and exploded.

That was a very real risk after the metaphorically runaway triumph of *Pickwick* (serialised April 1836–November 1837), soaring, as the numbered parts did, from an unviable 400 a month to an unprecedented 40,000. Busted boilers, along with other risks, were a regular peril in early train travel (*see* 'Trains').

Publishers can also crash. Chapman & Hall took a huge risk with *Pickwick*, and hoped for loyalty in return. They hoped in vain. Between August 1836 and July 1840, Dickens signed some ten agreements (each for progressively larger sums) with a rival publisher, Richard Bentley.

Bentley aimed, as Dickens perceived, to 'net' him. He was not an author easily trapped, even by a publisher as wily as 'the brigand of Burlington Street', as he was soon calling his new employer.

Most of the Bentley contracts related to the new journal, *Bentley's Miscellany*, which could as well have been called 'Boz, Boz and more Boz'. It would take off with a serialised foundling tale very different from *Pickwick*: *Oliver Twist*.

In April 1836, before the *Pickwick* triumph, Dickens had contracted with another publisher, John Macrone, for a three-volume novel. Macrone had brought out the reprint of the second series of *Sketches by Boz*, which had done well for both men. Dickens blithely transferred the commitment to write this novel to Bentley, for ten times the sum Macrone had offered. Bentley, however, would never see it. *Barnaby Rudge* (a historical novel – Dickens changing his tune yet again) eventually saw the light of print serialised in *Master Humphrey's Clock*, a threepenny weekly miscellany of Dickens's own, launched with Chapman & Hall in 1840. *The Old Curiosity Shop* (his most extended exercise in pathos, with the death of Little Nell Trent) was also serialised in *Master Humphrey's Clock*. From April 1838 to October 1839, Chapman & Hall had brought out *Nicholas Nickleby* in monthly parts: sales touched 70,000 a month.

In 1836 Dickens was a newly married, 24-year-old 'penny a liner', picking up what hack-work he could in Fleet Street. Aged 29 he was the most famous author in England, rich, courted by publishers with thousands in their hand, and seen by the population at large as a great man. In 1841 he was invited to stand for Parliament (he declined).

A meteor would have been jealous. This ferocious energy, and restless change of literary tune, is the pattern throughout his life. His boiler was never safe from the pressure he put on it. He would eventually burst it, dying prematurely in 1870 from an aneurysm in the brain (an explosion in the head).

✎ Candles ✎

'Butcher, baker, candlestick maker'. Why, in this Victorian trio, was the chandler up there along with two purveyors of the staffs-of-life?

The answer requires an act of readerly imagination. We inhabit a world with light at the fingertips. Fingers and lights meant different things in Dickens's world. 'Pickwick' was a name differently loaded for the Victorian reader (for us it has a slightly uncomfortable genital reference). Samuel's surname recalls the commonest kind of domestic light: a floating wick in tallow. The pesky wick would drown and need to be delicately 'picked' out and, if necessary, 'trimmed' (there were special scissors for doing this, and other special scissors for snuffing candles).

Tallow – mutton fat – was used for cheaper illumination. It smelled. Wax was expensive and didn't smell. In *Great Expectations*, Miss Havisham leaves Camilla ('Mrs Camels') £5 in her will for rushlights. What are they? The cheapest available candles – rush plants dipped in tallow. Very smelly.

And very unreliable: Dickens makes a little jest on the subject in *Edwin Drood* about the six little brothers who have predeceased the Rev. Septimus Crisparkle and who 'went out, one by one, as they were born, like six little rushlights as they were lighted'. Not a brilliant jest – but Dickens's readers would have got it better than we do.

When Magwitch returns, late at night, Pip is reading. With what? A reading lamp (oil-fuelled). He picks it up to get a closer look at his visitor. It would have thrown a dim, 'gentle' light, adding to the mystery of the scene.

Again in *Great Expectations*, why are Jaggers's office candles 'fat'? Because his clerks work at their desks after nightfall. Fat wax candles meant they wouldn't constantly have to be getting up to replace the things. The alternative would be candelabra. But they were too fussy for a workplace. Leave them to genteel drawing and dining rooms, where servants could do the necessary.

Lighting the many nightly candles in the kind of house Dickens lived in after he made his name was complicated. You needed first of all to light a taper with a not always reliable phosphorus match, then go round any number of wicks.

When the constables mount a posse to hunt down the escaped convict Magwitch on the marshes they have torches – bundles of twigs dunked in pitch or tar. In towns these 'links' were illuminated in metal holders by 'link boys'. On foggy nights in London, they would go round the streets offering their services. When, at the climax of *Great Expectations*, the metropolitan police again appear to arrest Magwitch, they will have bull's-eye, oil-fired, hand lamps.

One could go on. The main point is that the Victorian reader visualised, more precisely than we ever can, the varying light-effects in Dickens's fiction. They also smelled the lighted scene differently (snuffed candles, for example, whether wax or tallow, threw off a nauseating, if brief, scent).

Dickens associated candles with death. He talks, for instance, of the 'shroud' – the solidifying coils, rings, and ridges of molten wax made as it dripped and creased down the candle stem. Candles were indeed life-threatening – a major source of household fires. Every reader of *Great Expectations* will recall the vivid scene of Miss Havisham ablaze:

> I saw a great flaming light spring up. In the same moment, I saw her running at me, shrieking, with a whirl of fire blazing all about her, and soaring at least as many feet above her head as she was high.

We see a burning woman. Victorians, I suspect, would have seen a human candle. Some might even have glanced uneasily at the very candle they were reading Mr Dickens's novel by.

Between the first and last of Dickens's novels there were big changes in domestic and public lighting. The first gas lamps are mentioned in *Great Expectations*. *Edwin Drood*'s indoor night scenes are bathed in warm oil-lamp light, texturally different from what would have illumined the Pickwick Club dinners. Artificial light, like daylight, has a multitude of characters in Dickens's fiction.

By candlelight: *Bleak House*.

❧ Cane ❧

If there was a biblical proverb dear to the Victorian heart it was 'spare the rod and spoil the child'. Corporal punishment was given a ceremonial *dignitas* by the 'rod' itself, or cane (whose flexibility caused exquisite pain but did not, like a stiff stick, break bones), which also served as a baton signifying author-ity, as with Mrs Joe's fearsome 'Tickler' in *Great Expectations*. This instrument of righteous chastisement, as implacable as the sword of justice in the hand of the female statue on the Old Bailey, first makes an appearance in the text after Pip has returned (cul-pably late) from his traumatic encounter with Magwitch on the marshes. The Tickler ('a wax-ended piece of cane, worn smooth by collision with my tickled frame') is scarcely less terrifying than Magwitch's imaginary 'other young man' who eats boys' livers – although the Tickler aims for a different part of the infant anatomy.

David Copperfield's first experience of the cane is at the hands of Mr Murdstone, who has no intention of spoiling the step-child he has taken on. His rod is no mere tickler:

One morning when I went into the parlour with my books, I found my mother looking anxious, Miss Murdstone looking firm, and Mr Murdstone binding something round the bottom of a cane – a lithe and limber cane, which he left off binding when I came in, and poised and switched in the air.

A split cane lessens the pain. David finally fights back with his teeth, and is sent off to Mr Creakle's school. The master is intro-duced, rod-first:

Mr Creakle came to where I sat, and told me that if I were famous for biting, he was famous for biting, too. He then showed me the cane, and asked me what I thought of THAT, for a tooth? Was it a sharp tooth, hey? Was it a double tooth, hey? Had it a deep prong, hey? Did it bite, hey? Did it bite? At every question he gave me a fleshy cut with it that made me writhe ...

Mr Creakle's flogging, as George Orwell noted, has a clear sexual element. He cannot, we are told, resist a 'chubby' boy – buttocks are implied. One of the rituals of the 'proper caning' was the bare bum. Creakle will enjoy that, at his leisure, in his study. And his flagellation goes well beyond chastisement into grievous bodily harm, as with poor Traddles. He should be in prison. It's an odd gratuitous concession in Dickens's narrative that he ends up a magistrate.

The champion caner in Dickens's fiction is the aptly named Wackford Squeers. His cane ever to hand (and followed around by his sister with two spares), Squeers flogs anything in short trousers. Boys will be boys and boys will be flogged; Bolder, for example, for having warts on his hand.

Ignoring the child's excuse – 'They will come' – and with the vague justification that they must surely be masturbatory in origin, Wackford gets to whacking:

'Bolder,' said Squeers, tucking up his wristbands, and moistening the palm of his right hand to get a good grip of the cane, 'you're an incorrigible young scoundrel, and as the last thrashing did you no good, we must see what another will do towards beating it out of you.'

With this, and wholly disregarding a piteous cry for mercy, Mr Squeers fell upon the boy and caned him soundly: not leaving off, indeed, until his arm was tired out.

Did Dickens cane his remiss sons? Probably, yes. Probably not too hard.

Wackford whacked.

ᙍ Cannibalism ᙍ

'Thackeray and Cannibalism' would be a very thin volume. There's just the ballad 'Little Billee' and a couple of jokes about the possibly mythical Sawney Bean's cannibalistic Scottish clan (fed up with porridge and haggis, they feasted on human flesh). A book on George Eliot and cannibalism would have nothing between its covers but blank pages. Harry Stone, however, finds enough in Dickens and cannibalism to furnish a vastly entertaining monograph (*The Nightside of Dickens*).

Like most children, Dickens was introduced to 'the unpardonable sin' by gruesome fairy stories such as 'Jack and the Beanstalk'. He found added fuel for his fascination in *The Terrific Register*, a weekly 'penny dreadful' that he came across aged twelve. It made him, he said, 'unspeakably miserable', and frightened 'my very wits out of my head'. But he eagerly spent his penny a week for the latest issue, 'in which there was always a pool of blood, and at least one body'. Sometimes more than one, as in the *Register*'s description of the cannibalistic Sawney Bean family (accompanied by a graphic woodcut):

> The Men had their privy members thrown into the fire, their hands and legs were severed from their bodies, and they were permitted to bleed to death. The wretched mother of the whole crew, the daughters and grandchildren, after being spectators of the death of the men, were cast into three separate fires, and consumed to ashes.

Strong stuff for a twelve-year-old.

In the early 1850s Dickens wrote four essays on cannibalism for *Household Words*. The ostensible subject was the shipwreck of the Sir John Franklin expedition, which embarked for the Arctic in 1845 and was never heard of again. A few remains were found that suggested the crew had resorted to cannibalism. Dickens refused to accept the fact. It must, he argued, have been eskimos. Civilised men could never stoop to eating civilised men.

In Dickens's first published novel, *The Pickwick Papers*, there is a hilarious scene in which two medical students come into the dining room where the hero is eating his Christmas dinner:

'Nothing like dissecting, to give one an appetite,' said Mr Bob Sawyer, looking round the table.

Mr Pickwick slightly shuddered.

'By the bye, Bob,' said Mr Allen, 'have you finished that leg yet?'

'Nearly,' replied Sawyer, helping himself to half a fowl as he spoke. 'It's a very muscular one for a child's.'

'Is it?' inquired Mr Allen carelessly.

'Very,' said Bob Sawyer, with his mouth full.

On the marshes in *Great Expectations*, the starving Magwitch feels Pip's very unmuscular cheeks with the ruminative comment: 'Darn me, if I couldn't eat 'em.' He has with him, he says, a young companion who rather prefers livers.

In Dickens's last novel, *Edwin Drood*, there is the following description of Rochester ('Cloisterham'):

A monotonous, silent city, deriving an earthy flavour throughout from its Cathedral crypt, and so abounding in vestiges of monastic graves, that the Cloisterham children grow small salad in the dust of abbots and abbesses, and make dirt-pies of nuns and friars; while every ploughman in its outlying fields renders to once puissant Lord Treasurers, Archbishops, Bishops, and such-like, the attention which the Ogre in the story-book desired to render to his unbidden visitor, and grinds their bones to make his bread.

Dickens, one suspects, never so much as ate a slice of bread and butter without thinking, cannibalistically, of those ground-up bones.

৵ Carlylism ৶

Thomas Carlyle is the dedicatee of *Hard Times* and the Scottish sage's grim strictures can be tracked everywhere in Dickens's snow. Dickens agreed passionately with Carlyle's view that society should be organic, not mechanical. Famously, it was the two cartloads of books borrowed from the London Library that the great historian sent round to his house, Dickens claimed, that made possible *A Tale of Two Cities*.

In point of fact, as editors point out, it was a single text – 'Mr Carlyle's wonderful book', *The French Revolution* (1837) – that is the primary source for Dickens's tale.

It was not merely Carlyle's political analysis (effectively 'mistreat people badly enough and they will bite back') but the Carlylean rhetoric that inspired Dickens to emulation. Compare the following two descriptions of the storming of the Bastille. Who wrote which?

Cannon, *muskets*, fire and smoke; but, still the deep ditch, the single drawbridge, *the massive stone walls*, and the eight great towers. Slight displacements of *the raging sea*, made by the falling wounded. Flashing weapons, blazing torches, smoking waggonloads of wet straw, hard work at neighbouring barricades in all directions, shrieks, volleys, *execrations*, bravery without stint, boom smash and rattle, and the furious sounding of *the living sea*; but, still the deep ditch, and *the single drawbridge*, and the *massive stone walls*, and the eight great towers …

Ever wilder swells *the tide of men*; their infinite hum wax-
ing ever louder, into imprecations, perhaps into crackle of stray
musketry, – which latter, on *walls nine feet thick*, cannot do
execution. *The Outer Drawbridge* has been lowered for Thuriot;
new deputation of citizens (it is the third, and noisiest of all)
penetrates that way into the Outer Court ... A slight sputter; –
which has kindled the too combustible chaos; made it a roaring
fire-chaos! Bursts forth insurrection, at sight of its own blood
(for there were deaths by that sputter of fire), into endless rolling
explosion of *musketry*, distraction, *execration*.

[My italics]

It's hot air, but, to re-use Dickens's word, 'wonderful'.

Dickens hero-worshipped Carlyle. He told John Forster: 'I
would go at all times farther to see Carlyle than any man alive.'
Carlyle – despite the civil cartloads of useful reading matter –
would not go so far. As he confided to Charles Kingsley:

Dickens ... was a good little fellow, and one of the most cheery,
innocent natures he had ever encountered ... His theory of life
was entirely wrong. He thought men ought to be buttered up,
and the world made soft and accommodating for them, and
all sorts of fellows have turkey for their Christmas dinner ...
Dickens had not written anything which would be found of
much use in solving the problems of life.

Not even *Hard Times*, Thomas?

(PS. Dickens's is the first passage.)

Paris riots.

↩ **Catholicism** ↪

This entry could as well be called 'Papistry'. Dickens was sufficiently prejudiced against Rome for the insulting term to fit. As
Humphry House records:

> Among the false-book backs with which he decorated his study
> at Gad's Hill was a set called: 'The Wisdom of our Ancestors' –
> I. *Ignorance*. II. *Superstition*. III. *The Block*. IV. *The Stake*. V. *The
> Rack*. VI. *Dirt*. VII. *Disease*.

Four of those seven could be subsumed under the single word
'Rome'.

For Dickens the Reformation was something much more
liberating than the French Revolution – which had misguidedly
stormed the Bastille rather than Notre Dame. As Robert Newsom
puts it:

> Dickens was perfectly convinced that Roman Catholicism
> embodied the worst evils of the past, that it was the epitome of
> ignorance and superstition, slavish obedience to priestly author-
> ity … Only a few months before his death, in a letter to John
> Forster, he referred to Roman Catholicism as 'that curse upon
> the world'.

Dickens unleashed his contempt in *Pictures from Italy*, the travel
book whose prejudices have made it among the least popular of
his works. Particularly in Italy. His distaste for all things Roman
distorted his perception, as in the following:

On Sunday, the Pope assisted in the performance of High Mass at St Peter's. The effect of the Cathedral on my mind, on that second visit, was exactly what it was at first, and what it remains after many visits. It is not religiously impressive or affecting. It is an immense edifice, with no one point for the mind to rest upon; and it tires itself with wandering round and round.

He goes on to sneer at the 'black statue of St Peter ... under a red canopy; which is larger than life and which is constantly having its great toe kissed by good Catholics'. So much for Arnolfo di Cambio and Michelangelo.

Paradoxically, the novel Dickens published three years earlier is more temperate. *Barnaby Rudge* (1841) climaxes on the 'No Popery' riots of 1780: a violent popular reaction to a mild Catholic Relief bill, designed to lift prejudicial obstructions from some areas of English public life.

The riot was instigated, as Dickens narrates it, by mad Lord George Gordon and his sinister *aide de camp*, Gashford. The mob ('the very scum and refuse of London') is led by a hangman, the brutal bastard son of a corrupt nobleman, and an idiot with a pet raven on his shoulder croaking: 'I'm a devil, I'm a Polly, I'm a kettle, I'm a Protestant, No Popery!' Vox populi, vox parrot.

The novel makes clear that however much Dickens disliked 'the Romish Church' and all that toe-kissing, he disliked rioters much much more.

ｃ๑ Cats ๑ɔ

Dickens created the most horrible cat in fiction outside the furry horrors of Edgar Allan Poe – namely Lady Jane in *Bleak House*, the familiar of the rag and bone merchant Krook (witches, third nipples and cloven feet are distantly evoked). She lies in wait perpetually for Miss Flite to drop her guard so that the innocent madwoman's caged larks, linnets and finches may be torn feather from feather and devoured – 'allegory', as Dickens unnecessarily reminds the reader, for what may await Ada and Richard, those two orphans, adrift in the world, who come under the care of Mr Jarndyce.

Whenever she appears, Lady Jane – a great grey beast with green eyes and tigerish claws – snarls, bares her teeth, and threatens. Her favourite position is on Krook's shoulder. Luckily she's not there when he spontaneously combusts – or perhaps she used the second of her nine lives. She has already used the first, as Krook tells the appalled Esther:

> I deal in cat-skins among other general matters, and hers was offered to me. It's a very fine skin, as you may see, but I didn't have it stripped off!

Jane was not a name Dickens liked: he bestows it on the most detestable woman in all his fiction, Jane Murdstone. As a slang term 'Lady Jane' is recorded as meaning either 'prostitute' or 'vagina'. I suspect Dickens knew that, and gambled that his lady and young readers wouldn't (*see* 'Nomenclature').

On the evidence of his fiction Dickens was not a cat person. The swindler, seducer and cold-blooded sadist Carker's smile, in *Dombey and Son*, 'has something in it of the snarl of a cat'. Best not to be a mouse when Mr Carker is around. Nonetheless we have it on good testimony that towards the end of his life Dickens relaxed his felinophobia and even came to be fond of the beast he once disliked.

Cats were banned from his London houses, as his daughter Mamie records, because of Dickens's beloved birds (*see* 'Ravens'). He was entirely with Miss Flite in this regard. But when he took up residence in Gad's Hill in 1860, there was enough space to enlarge his menagerie and the birds he loved were outside, in the 25-acre grounds. Mamie recalls receiving from a friend in London

> a present of a white kitten – Williamina … she showed particular devotion to my father. I remember on one occasion when she had presented us with a family of kittens, she selected a corner of father's study for their home. … One of these kittens was kept, who, as he was quite deaf, was left unnamed, and became known by the servants as 'the master's cat,' because of his devotion to my father. He was always with him, and used to follow him about the garden like a dog, and sit with him while he wrote.

This was presumably the cat, Bob, named after Bob Cratchit. Dickens had Bob's paw (Krook would have approved) made into the handle of his letter-opener (one of Cratchit's daily tasks) when the beast died in 1862. The object went on display at the 100th anniversary exhibition of the New York Public Library in 2011.

⮑ Cauls ⮐

The first note in every annotated edition of *David Copperfield* throws light on the sentence that begins the fourth paragraph:

> I was born with a caul, which was advertised for sale, in the newspapers, at the low price of fifteen guineas.

As Andrew Sanders explains it, in the Oxford World's Classics edition:

> The caul is the membrane which encloses the foetus before birth. It was superstitiously believed that the possessor of a caul was safe from drowning.

Although not a nautical novelist like Captain Marryat, the caul reference witnesses the fact that Dickens was born by the sea, spent formative childhood years among the country's principal Navy yards, and spent many of his later years along the sea. It's instructive to draw up a list of characters in his fiction who undergo drowning, near-drowning, or supposed drowning. One can stress the salience of watery death by cross-reference to its infrequency in other major Victorian novelists.

In the fiction of the Brontë sisters, only one major character may be thought to have died at sea: Paul Emanuel in *Villette*.

In Thackeray no major character drowns.

In Hardy's *The Return of the Native* two characters die by drowning, and Newson in *The Mayor of Casterbridge* and Troy in *Far From the Madding Crowd* are presumed drowned.

In George Eliot, Maggie and Tom Tulliver drown at the end of *The Mill on the Floss*.

Dickens's list is longer by far: Quilp, John Harmon, Walter Gay, Lady Dedlock, Rogue Magwitch and Compeyson (*see* 'Compeyson's Hat') all have life-changing encounters with water. Edwin Drood, in Dickens's last novel, is supposed drowned. 'The sea, Floy, what is it that it keeps saying?' Paul Dombey asks his sister, as he regards the waves from his bath chair at the beach. No answer is forthcoming – but nothing very friendly, we deduce. Like Mr Dombey's train, the sinister echo is 'Death' (*see* 'Trains').

The Old Curiosity Shop is famous for the unjustly sneered-at death of Little Nell. In fact it is the drowning death of Quilp (her would-be seducer) that is the more brilliant piece of writing in that novel.

> One loud cry, now – but the resistless water bore him down before he could give it utterance, and, driving him under it, carried away a corpse … It toyed and sported with its ghastly freight, now bruising it against the slimy piles, now hiding it in mud or long rank grass, now dragging it heavily over rough stones and gravel, now feigning to yield it to its own element, and in the same action luring it away, until, tired of the ugly plaything, it flung it on a swamp – a dismal place where pirates had swung in chains through many a wintry night – and left it there to bleach.

Where is that caul when you need it?

The death of Quilp.

✦ Charity ✦

The Victorians had no welfare state as such – and they had many
more of the population in need of welfare. There were the parochial
workhouses, of course, institutions going back to the Elizabethan
era which, in an age of mass movement, could no longer cope.
Dickens observed that any rational person would break a window
and go to prison (where the ration allowances were twice as gener-
ous) as willingly as put themselves under the care of beadles like
Oliver Twist's Mr Bumble in the local workhouse.

Charity, it was believed, would do what institutions could not
do, or would only do cruelly. The novel in which Dickens ponders
charity and its problems from every possible angle is *Bleak House*.
Ada and Richard in that novel are wards of court, Esther is an
unwanted orphan. All three are dependent, utterly, on the discreet
charity of Mr Jarndyce. A fatherly figure, he effectively adopts
them.

But is Jarndyce right in extending that same adoptive charity to
the wholly unworthy Skimpole – the false child, who bamboozles
his benefactor shamefully? In his own charitable venture, Urania
Cottage (*see* 'Home for the Homeless'), Dickens was assiduous in
interviewing candidate fallen women to sniff out any potential
Skimpolism.

Legal adoption (as Betsey Trotwood adopts David Copperfield)
is genuinely charitable in Dickens's world. But so, too, is pseudo-
adoption: as happens between David and Traddles, or between
Nicholas Nickleby and Smike, or between Brownlow and Oliver
Twist.

This kind of relationship reproduces ideal family relationships
as 'step' relationships (Murdstone and David, for example) never
do with Dickens. Esther, having risen to the post of mistress of

Bleak House – but not, of course, mistress of its owner – takes on Charley (and through her the parentless children she cares for) and Caddy, as unfortunate younger sisters. She reproduces what has made her a success in life in so doing. Woodcourt, Snagsby and Rouncewell (and before them Nemo) are admirable for their casual charities towards Jo the Sweeper. A grown-up indigent would be a less worthy object of charity, although why is hard to say.

Charity, as the Victorian proverb insisted, begins at home. The further away it is, as with Mrs Jellyby's 'telescopic philanthropy' in *Bleak House*, or Mr Honeythunder's 'Convened Chief Composite Committee of Central and District Philanthropists' in *Edwin Drood*, the more distorted and less genuinely charitable it will become.

There is, however, an example elsewhere of telescopic philanthropy that is vexingly contradictory. In *Great Expectations*, Magwitch earns a fortune honestly in Australia, the bulk of which he remits, charitably, to Pip. He is reproducing, on a huge scale, the infant Pip's bringing him a charitable pork pie, rather than shopping him (as duty demands) to the police fifteen years earlier. But why, when he discovers the source of his great expectations, does Pip spurn Magwitch's money – preferring poverty and a drudging career as (horror!) a clerk? Why is the reformed Magwitch's sheep-farming cash less acceptable than Miss Havisham's brewery fortune? It's not easy to come up with an answer to that question, and Dickens does not try.

∽ Cheap Dickens ∾

Dickens's 'profile' in his heyday was phenomenal. He was in the very air his contemporaries breathed. How was it achieved without the communication technologies (TV, film, celebrity magazines) that we have?

'Steam' is the answer. Dickens's fiction, more than any other writer before him, benefited from the railway networks that spread over the whole of Britain following the 'railway mania' of the late 1830s and early 1840s. The latest number of *Dombey and Son* – for example, that dealing with Mr Dombey's rail trip to Leamington – was probably read on railway journeys from the magnificent new Euston terminus to Leamington.

Steam-propelled Dickens ran even faster in the 1850s when W.H. Smith ('First with the News') capitalised on the railway system to get their highly perishable materials out the same way. Railway mania was good for Dickens. It enabled him to pulse out his latest novel, via Smith's and the railways, to every corner of the kingdom. The serial parts and magazines in which his work was printed went out on 'magazine day', at the end of the week and the month. His twopenny journals went out on Thursdays, weekly. And his Christmas books were distributed, at high speed, for the country to enjoy over the winter holidays. His huge sales fitted, hand in glove, with Bradshaw's famous train timetable.

His new novels sold like hot cakes. But how to capitalise on the less-than-new Dickens titles? The mass-market paperback was a century off. How to 'work the back-list' and make those old cakes hot again? Dickens's first publishers, Chapman & Hall, who had risen up like the stick on the soaring Boz rocket, hit on a solution. In 1847 they launched their 'Cheap Edition' of Dickens's now substantial corpus of fiction and non-fiction. The way it worked was, truly, revolutionary. The author had prudently kept a hold on his copyrights. His books were broken into 'particles' costing a penny-halfpenny each. It was newspaper price – and the parts were available, like newspapers, at stalls as well as bookshops. Railway stalls, principally.

Martin Chuzzlewit, a book less than three years old in March 1847, would cost a Cheap Edition subscriber four shillings in 32 weekly issued three-halfpence parts. *Oliver Twist*, on the same terms, came in at a bargain half-crown (two shillings and sixpence – 25p in our currency). The result was what a modern advertising agency would recognise as 'total Dickens'. All his work, country-wide, was now available simultaneously at near-giveaway price. Dickens here, Dickens there, Dickens everywhere. Chapman & Hall were soon printing millions of parts a year. How did their presses cope? By steam. Just like the railways or the Manchester cotton mills.

Dickens waxed lyrical about 'Cheap Dickens' in the advertisement for the venture:

> It had been intended that this CHEAP EDITION should not be undertaken until the books were much older, or the Author was dead … To become in his new guise, a permanent inmate of many English homes … and to see and feel this – not to die first, or grow old and passionless, must obviously be among the hopes of a *living* author, venturing on such an enterprise.

No author 'lived' as vitally, or omnipresently. 'Cheap', it will be clear, was not, in the 1840s, a term of abuse. 'Cheap and proud of it' was the motto. None prouder than Dickens.

⌒ Cheek ⌒

(Not) bringing a blush to a young person's cheek (particularly the 'maiden' cheek) is one of many phrases to have broken free of Dickens's fiction to live a life of its own in popular discourse.

It originates in Chapter 13 of *Our Mutual Friend* as the quintessence, double-distilled, of Podsnappery straight from the Podsnap mouth:

> 'I would say,' added Mr Podsnap, looking round upon his compatriots, and sounding solemnly with his theme, 'that there is in the Englishman a combination of qualities, a modesty, an independence, a responsibility, a repose, combined with an absence of everything calculated to call a blush into the cheek of a young person, which one would seek in vain among the Nations of the Earth.'

In the way of Dickensian characterisation, that sacred cheek becomes an identifying parrot call. Here comes that fool Podsnap again, we feel, with his damned cheek.

This pompous blowhard is often claimed to be an unkind portrait of John Forster. It may well be. But it's also, in an odd way, a portrait of the artist himself in middle age, and an expression of something that made him uneasy as an artist in his maturity. One thinks of Flaubert's 'Madame Bovary, c'est moi'.

Dickens's earlier fiction is much more likely to bring out the tell-tale blush than his later, which moves, discreetly, in the opposite direction. Take the strange business of Magwitch's marriage in *Great Expectations*. Dickens goes well out of the way his narrative is taking to insert a little back-story recording that Magwitch was married to his 'Missis' by an 'over the broomstick' ceremony. That the reprobate would have married a doxy quite likely to have given her sexual favours to his worst enemy is wholly unlikely. Why did Dickens bother? Because he wanted to legitimise and decontaminate Estella, later revealed as Magwitch's daughter. That fragrant young person should not have the whiff of illicit sex about her.

Podsnappery.

Dickens, if not quite a novelist of two cities, spent a lot of time in Paris. As his letters testify, he taught himself fluent French. He would certainly have taken notice of what was going on across the Channel in 1857, the year of prosecution in which Flaubert's *Madame Bovary*, Baudelaire's *Les Fleurs du Mal*, and Eugène Sue's *Les Mystères de Paris* were hauled into court on the charge of *outrage aux bonnes moeurs* (offence to public decency). All were cleared, creating a new zone of freedom for French writers, whose fiction duly roared ahead of the English and American variety.

British society had gone in quite the opposite direction. An Act brought forward by Lord Campbell for the first time codified censorship in that same momentous year, 1857. As laid down by British law, the criterion was not 'public decency' but any 'tendency to deprave and corrupt' (young persons, principally).

However he might crucify Podsnap with his satire, Dickens went along with the new moral conformities, although a writer with his immense authority could have rebelled – as lesser writers like George Moore did – and affronted the young person's cheek when art required it. It would, of course, have been risky and would have hit his pocket and his reputation. With his mistress Ellen Ternan in the background he had other reasons for being cautious. Moore's novels were banned from the country's largest lending library, Mudie's, and Hardy's *Jude the Obscure* was burned by a bishop. The publisher, Henry Vizetelly, was sent to prison for publishing Emile Zola's novels in the 1880s. It killed him. There was little pity. He had, *The Times* said, thrown a vial of acid in the public's face (that cheek again).

Dickens submitted to the rule of Podsnap. None of his novels offended. It caused him, one may be sure, inner doubt. But he was, after all, English.

✌ Child Abuse ∾

There is a lot of it in Dickens's fiction. It sticks in the mind long after the book has been put down. Oliver, starved. Smike brain-damaged. Traddles and David whipped like curs, Nell hunted to death like an animal – say 'Dickens' and the images come crowding in.

In only one very minor way may we charge Dickens himself with child abuse: with respect, namely, to the names he affixed to his luckless male offspring. Of one thing we may be sure. It was he, not his wife Kate, who came up with them (she may have been permitted the wholly innocuous girls' names – Mary, Kate, etc.).

Charles Culliford Boz Dickens (b. 1847) was the couple's first-born male child. Why 'Boz'? Because, legend has it, someone arriving late to the christening saw Dickens and shouted it out as a greeting. The parson misheard it as an instruction.

Being his father's namesake, twice over, was a hard burden for 'Charley' (he failed in life, like all but one of Dickens's sons). The second-born son, Walter Landor Dickens (b. 1841), was named after a famous ('then famous', perhaps one should say) man of letters. So too with the next in line, Francis Jeffrey Dickens (b. 1844), named after the austere Scottish critic – the greatest of his time, Dickens thought. His son's views on the founder of the *Edinburgh Review* are not recorded. Alfred Tennyson D'Orsay Dickens (b. 1845), his fourth son, was named for what Michael Slater calls 'two bizarrely contrasting godfathers'. The lesser known was a dandy and the consort of the fashionable novelist, Countess Blessington. Sydney Smith Haldimand Dickens (b. 1847) was named after the wit who much amused Dickens. Haldimand was Dickens's compliment to a friend, William Haldimand, made in Switzerland in 1847. Next came Henry Fielding Dickens (b. 1849), so named, John Forster informs us, because Dickens was reading *Tom Jones* as he began *David Copperfield*. It was a happy omen. Henry went on to be the only one of Dickens's sons who can be said to have made a success of their lives, as one of the country's leading lawyers. None of the children, one notes, went into writing, despite their hyper-literary names.

Edward Bulwer-Lytton Dickens (b. 1852, nicknamed 'Plorn') was the last of Dickens's male offspring and was given his wholly grotesque name in tribute to the baronet novelist with whom Dickens was currently working on their charitable foundation for writers, The Guild of Literature and Art.

It is sometimes speculated that Dickens and his mistress Ellen Ternan had an illegitimate child who died. If so, what did they baptise the unfortunate infant, who is supposed to have been born in France? Gustave Flaubert Dickens perhaps?

✍ Children ✍

If one knows anything about Dickens it is that he was the first novelist to bring the child into the centre of British fiction. Say 'Dickens' and Tiny Tim is blessing us, Little Nell is expiring beautifully, and Oliver is plaintively asking for more. Dickens did for childhood what Wordsworth had done in poetry with his story of the 'seedtime of his soul', *The Prelude*. (If this were a PhD thesis, it would be tempting to examine the clear evidence in *Great Expectations* and *David Copperfield* that Dickens had steeped himself in Wordsworth's poetry before writing his most autobiographical works.)

Oddly, however, concern with the child is not present in the first novel Dickens conceived (*Barnaby Rudge* as it would be) or the first novel he published, *The Pickwick Papers*. What triggered his passionate interest thereafter in the infant? The question is easily answered. He married in April 1836, in the same month that the first instalment of *Pickwick* came into the world. His first child, Charles Dickens Jr (as Americans were to call him), followed nine months later, to the day. Little 'Charley' evidently brought back recollections of Dickens's own unhappy childhood and a resolution that his offspring would not suffer the same way.

Thereafter children came thick and fast – in his homes and into his narratives. He had a growing brood of children around him as he wrote: ten in all by 1852. They were not thinned out, as half his own siblings had been, by disease or neglect. That Dickens not only wrote about children, but cared for them, is borne out by their extraordinary survival rate for young Victorians.

After Dickens parted from his wife, in 1860, children figure less and less prominently. *Edwin Drood*, for example, is a childless

Waiting for father: *Our Mutual Friend*.

narrative, apart from the 'hideous small boy in rags' who flings stones at Durdles. He is not loveable.

In his middle years, Dickens is more concerned with adolescence (although the term had not been yet invented). Amy Dorrit (*Little Dorrit*) and Bella Wilfer (*Our Mutual Friend*) are on the verge of 'majority', as are the quartet of young people at the centre of *Drood*. Dickens, as the years passed, had preponderantly older children: career and marriage were now the issues.

Dickens died prematurely with decades of work still inside him. His interests in fiction are keyed in with his time of life. One aches for the fiction he could have written about what it is to be old.

✍ Christmas ✍

Two Victorians are responsible for the rituals of our modern British Christmas. One was the German husband of the Queen. Prince Albert it was who replaced the venerable Anglo-Saxon Yule log with the alien Teutonic *Weihnachtsbaum* – or 'Christmas Tree'.

The second Victorian is the author of *The Pickwick Papers*. It was, plausibly, Dickens who remodelled the British Christmas into an annual orgy of benevolence, or, as Scrooge's nephew puts it in *A Christmas Carol*:

> [T]he only time ... in the long calendar of the year, when men and women seem by one consent to open their shut-up hearts freely, and to think of people below them as if they really were fellow-passengers to the grave ...

Dickens himself steps forward in the famous Dingley Dell Christmas chapter in *Pickwick* to sermonise along the same lines.

Christmas, we are instructed, is our foretaste, no less, of heaven which awaits the truly benevolent after death:

> [A] source of such pure and unalloyed delight … that the religious belief of the most civilised nations, and the rude traditions of the roughest savages, alike number it among the first joys of a future condition of existence, provided for the blessed and happy.

Ah, sneered the clever French critic, Louis Cazamian, 'la philosophie de Noël', with the implication of 'quelle simplesse'. Dickens was, as his bank account demonstrated, no simpleton about the commercial opportunities of the festival of 'unalloyed delight' when wallets, less clamped than Scrooge's were loosened.

He invented the 'Christmas Book' (Scrooge's story is the first), to be marketed in December as a gift. The invention proved an annual gold mine, as did the swollen 'Christmas Editions' of his two papers, *Household Words* and *All the Year Round*. For Dickens, the literary businessman, Christmas was a time of receiving as much as giving.

As careful readers will note in the above quotes, there is a visitor at the Dickensian festive board with a hood on his head and a scythe over his shoulder. 'Happy journey to our grave, my fellow passengers!' It's not a toast to rival Tiny Tim's 'God bless us every one'.

But everything Dickens wrote, carefully regarded, is bordered by black – like the in-mourning writing paper the Victorians used when one of the family died. Consider the opening chapter of *Great Expectations*. It's Christmas Eve. Pip is together, as families should be on that sacred occasion, with his mother, father, and five siblings. They, however, are under their gravestones. It's a

Bob Cratchit's Christmas cheer.

Christmas party of one. Dickens, as *Great Expectations* was taking form in his mind, confided to John Forster that it would be 'comic' and 'exceedingly droll'.

If so, this would seem a very dark kind of comedy he had in mind, or, to mangle the song, 'I'm dreaming of a black Christmas'.

༄ **Circumlocution** ༄

There was a lot of military action – most of it related to the expansion and defence of Empire – but only one war worthy of the name during Dickens's lifetime. That war was 'The Crimean', in one of those far-off countries of which, as in other big wars, the British population knew little.

Britain and her allies won. Celebratory 'Crimean cannon', ordnance won from Johnny Turk and the Russian Bear, still stand as defensive bollards to keep cars off the pavements in London's Soho.

Dickens hated Russia (the home of serfdom) and cheered the bravery of 'our valiant men' at Balaclava and other battles as loudly as any other patriot. He was, however, enraged to the point of explosion by the monumental cock-up that the War Office, and Whitehall, produced logistically. 'Red Tapism', as he called it, killed more gallant Britons than the enemy (among whom, interestingly, was Leo Tolstoy – reading at the time Thackeray, not Dickens).

Dickens threw his formidable energies into propagandising for the Administrative Reform Association. After the war, in his next novel, *Little Dorrit* (December 1855–June 1857), he continued the assault with extended satire against the 'Circumlocution Office' and its exasperating mantra: 'Nobody's Fault'. The Civil Service was in 1855 ripe for reform. It was riddled with nepotism. Dickens satirised that particular corruption as the

> Family that controls the Circumlocution Office, where everything goes round in circles, and nothing ever gets done. Includes Lord Decimus Tite Barnacle, his wife, Lady Jemima Bilberry, nephew Tite Barnacle, and his son Clarence Barnacle (Barnacle Junior) Etc. etc.

The Barnacles were soon to be prised off the ship of state by the 1855 Northcote–Trevelyan reforms, which introduced public examinations for entry and, it was hoped, careers forwarded by talent, not family connection. Anthony Trollope (who had got his place in the Post Office through a friendly Barnacle) heartily disapproved. He didn't much like *Little Dorrit*, either.

It is the guiding rule of the Circumlocution Office, Arthur Clennam discovers, 'never, on any account whatever to give a straightforward answer'. His interview with the Office (in the matter of Dorrit's interminable imprisonment) is abruptly cut short when, to his immense relief, Barnacle Jr discovers: 'Egad you haven't got an appointment'. Case closed. See you in a few months' time, Mr Clennam.

Sixty years later, the sociologist Max Weber argued that as it entered the modern period, European society moved from *Gemeinschaft* (community) to *Gesellschaft* (bureaucracy) as its organising system. Bureaucratic rationality was efficient, but had a chilling, dehumanising effect. As Weber put it:

> No machinery in the world functions so precisely as this apparatus. [It] reduces every worker to a cog in this bureaucratic machine and, seeing himself in this light, he will merely ask how to transform himself into a somewhat bigger cog. ... The passion for bureaucratisation drives us to despair.

There are innumerable places in Dickens where the modern reader will mutter, 'the more it changes ...'. Nowhere more so than in reading Chapter 10 of *Little Dorrit*, 'Nobody's Fault'. Where have you heard that recently? Whitehall?

✺ Compeyson's Hat ✺

I believe I was the first to point out a teasing puzzle in *Great Expectations*. The story has one of the most gripping openings in literature ('hook 'em with the first instalment' was always Dickens's motto as a serialist).

As the action opens Pip is solemnly contemplating the graves of his family. Suddenly, from behind the tombstone of his father leaps a monster:

> A fearful man, all in coarse gray, with a great iron on his leg. A man with no hat, and with broken shoes, and with an old rag tied round his head.

It's not until Chapter 42, and sixteen years later, that the reader learns the details of how the 'fearful man' – Abel Magwitch, future source of Pip's great expectations – escaped from the 'hulks', decommissioned Navy vessels converted to prisons, anchored well offshore. Floating Alcatrazes, they added a new dimension to Dr Johnson's bitter jest: 'No man will be a sailor who has contrivance enough to get himself into jail; for being in a ship is being in a jail, with the chance of being drowned.'

When he returns to England (at the risk of being hanged) Magwitch explains to Pip how he escaped. He found himself in the same prison ship as Compeyson, the man who had betrayed him. He attacked his foe and was thrown into the 'black-hole' – the punishment cell. As he tells Pip:

> 'The black-hole of that ship warn't a strong one, to a judge of black-holes that could swim and dive. I escaped to the shore,

and I was a hiding among the graves there, envying them as was in 'em and all over, when I first see my boy!'

For a middle-aged man and a heavy smoker, Magwitch must have been in truly excellent shape. Diving into the current-ridden Thames estuary on 24 December and swimming several hundred yards to the shore fully clothed is no mean athletic feat. Doing so weighed down with a 'great iron' on your ankle suggests super-human powers.

Nor, it would seem, is Magwitch unique. On his way to the graveyard with the required 'wittles' and file for Magwitch, Pip meets Compeyson, who had also gone overboard from the hulk. He 'was dressed in coarse gray, too, and had a great iron on his leg'. Like Magwitch, Compeyson must be a remarkable swimmer. Even more remarkable, in fact, Compeyson has 'a flat broad-brimmed low-crowned felt hat on'.

It's a pity that the world would have to wait until 1896 for the first Olympic games. Had they been held in 1811, Britain could confidently have expected gold and silver in the 100-metre swimming finals.

৵ Courvoisier (1.) ৶

Until they were made illegal in the 1860s, public hangings ('hang fairs') were one of the more popular 'entertainments of the people'. Tens of thousands would attend: whole families would make a picnic day of it. Children would be held aloft at the critical moment, a disgusted Dickens recorded, 'to see how the gallows toy worked'.

Only at one London hanging is it on record that two major novelists of the day were in attendance and a third major novelist's work was entered in evidence as a plea for mitigation. That was the execution of François-Benjamin Courvoisier.

Courvoisier, a Swiss valet, slit the throat of his 70-year-old master, Lord William Russell. The squalid deed was committed while the old man was lying in his bed. The motive was theft. It was an open and shut case after Russell's belongings were found in Courvoisier's possession. He was briskly tried, found guilty, and hanged outside Newgate Prison on 6 July 1840. Forty thousand Londoners turned up to watch as the warm summer morning broke.

Among them was Dickens and two male friends. He had initially been reluctant – but suddenly decided he would 'like to watch a scene like this'. The three men hired a room with a view (telescopes were to hand), and spent the night in it. Until the moment itself there was plenty to watch. Pickpocketing, dox-ies publicly serving clients, drunken pranks, pie men shouting their tasty wares, peddlers selling penny 'broadsides' containing Courvoisier's 'last words'.

As dawn broke, Dickens was surprised to see Thackeray below in the crowd, and called out to him. Thackeray was virulently opposed to capital punishment. He wrote a powerful piece on the event, 'Going to See a Man Hanged', for the next edition of *Fraser's Magazine*. He did not, in fact 'see' the man hanged but turned away at the moment of the drop. He left Newgate, Thackeray wrote, with a 'disgust for murder, but it was for the murder I saw done'. But was it the 'seeing' (i.e. the publicity of the public execution) or the extreme punishment itself that disgusted him?

Dickens wrote up his reactions much later, in 1846, in a piece for the *Daily News*. He, too, had been more disgusted with the crowd than the hanging itself:

I hoped for an instant, that there was some sense of Death and Eternity in the ˙cry of 'Hats off!' when the miserable wretch appeared: but I found, next moment, that they only raised it as they would at a play – to see the Stage better in the final scene.

These two eminently sane Victorians came to much the same conclusion. Capital punishment was, like sex, so ugly it should be kept out of view. But, of course, it would still have to be done. In private. There should be no more fun at the (hang) fair.

✎ Courvoisier (2.) ✎

The Courvoisier hanging was momentous for English fiction. Three major careers were bent out of, or into shape, by it – depending how one likes to look.

Most affected was William Harrison Ainsworth. After Dickens broke from the publisher Richard Bentley, Ainsworth had taken over as editor and star-serialist in *Bentley's Miscellany*. He had made his name with the so-called 'Newgate Novel' – crime fiction. Ainsworth enjoyed a terrific hit with *Jack Sheppard*, the story of a 'flash cove' hanged at Tyburn. It ran from January 1839 to February 1840 in *Bentley's*, illustrated by George Cruikshank. There were at least eight (unauthorised) dramatic versions and as many plagiarised versions for the semi-literate public. Many at the time would have backed Ainsworth against Dickens as the coming novelist.

Clutching at straws, Courvoisier claimed that it was reading *Jack Sheppard* that inspired his murder. The plea triggered a familiar English moral panic. Ainsworth's novel, thundered the papers, was a 'cut-throat's manual'. The charge was preposterous, but it

W. Harrison Ainsworth.

was taken seriously by Ainsworth who dropped Newgate material like a hot potato, and thereafter wrote tepid historical romances. His career went downhill. Boz had nothing to fear from the author of *The Tower of London*.

Thackeray, while waiting for Courvoisier to hang, observed girl prostitutes servicing clients in nearby alleyways. He commented, in his essay:

Bah! what figments these novelists tell us! Boz, who knows life well, knows that his Miss Nancy [in *Oliver Twist*] is the most

> unreal fantastical personage possible; no more like a thief's mistress than one of [pastoral painter Solomon] Gessner's shepherdesses resembles a real country wench. He dare not tell the truth concerning such young ladies.

The 'honest painter of human nature', he concluded, cannot touch such material 'and therefore, in fact, had better leave the picture alone altogether'. Which he duly did in his fiction. No whores in Thackeray, despite those 55,000 parading nightly on the streets of London.

The attack on himself, and Thackeray's half-heartedness about the 'truth' of fiction, infuriated Dickens. He hit back thunderously in a preface to the reprint of *Oliver Twist*: 'It is useless to discuss whether the conduct and character of the girl [Nancy] seems natural or unnatural, probable or improbable, right or wrong. IT IS TRUE.'

But in his heart he knew it wasn't TRUE. Whores with hearts of gold, prepared to sacrifice their lives for virtue, were few and far between on the streets of Victorian London. Dickens never retracted in print, but Thackeray's blow hit home. Behind the scenes he went on to help young women of Nancy's kind in his Urania Cottage venture (*see* 'Home for the Homeless').

A case could be made that François-Benjamin Courvoisier did more to change Victorian fiction than any literary critic of the time.

↫ Darwin ↬

An inventory was made of Dickens's library for auction after his death. It contained many interesting items. Among them was a second edition of Darwin's *On the Origin of Species*, published on 7 January 1860. Dickens evidently acquired it during the huge splash the book made after its publication in the last week of November 1859.

In the first instalment of *Great Expectations* (published 1 December 1860), Pip describes the gravestones of five of his brothers 'who gave up trying to get a living, exceedingly early in that universal struggle'. As every annotated edition of the novel instructs, the allusion is to the title of Chapter 3 of the *Origin*, 'Struggle for Existence'.

There are hints throughout the text of the novel that Dickens took elements of Darwinism on board (Pip and Herbert embarking on pugilistic struggle the moment they meet, for example). Whatever else, Dickens was exceptionally quick off the mark. Both he and Darwin, one notes, were members of the Athenaeum Club.

Elsewhere Dickens was similarly quick on the uptake. The opening paragraph of *Bleak House*, whose first monthly number was published in March 1852, offers a pen-picture of London wrapped in November gloom:

> Smoke lowering down from chimney-pots, making a soft black drizzle, with flakes of soot in it as big as full-grown snowflakes – gone into mourning, one might imagine, for the death of the sun.

This is a clear reference to the 'heat death of the universe'. The theory was first given firm scientific articulation by William Thomson, in his book *On a Universal Tendency in Nature to the Dissipation of Mechanical Energy*, in 1852 – at exactly the moment the first number of *Bleak House* hit the stands. Thomson outlined an early version of the second law of thermodynamics. Its central concept is that energy inevitably dissipates. It led to speculation about the 'death of the sun'.

Thomson's book is not in Dickens's library. I suspect he picked up its contents from magazines and club conversation and wasted no time working it into his fiction.

Books such as Darwin's and Thomson's must, one suspects, have shaken Dickens's faith in Genesis. It was probably never that strong. When he rewrote the Bible for his children (a quintessentially Dickensian act) as *The Life of our Lord*, in 1846–49, it was the New Testament, and its ethics, that he confined himself to. Dickens never took a public position on evolution. His private position is clear enough.

↷ Dead Babies ↶

The *enfant terrible* (as he then was) of English fiction, Martin Amis, published a blackly comic novel by this name in 1975. It was so called because dead babies were the one thing you could not make jokes (even 'sick' jokes) about. Everything else was fair game, but not dead babies. So Martin went ahead and did.

Of the many readers of Amis's novel few, one suspects, had ever seen one. Dickens, like most of *his* readers, one suspects, certainly had.

A late-life essay in his paper, *All the Year Round*, records a visit to the town of Chatham (diplomatically but unflatteringly renamed 'Dullborough') where Dickens had spent formative years as a child. 'In my very young days', he recalls being taken on a walk by his nurse, and

at a little greengrocer's shop, down certain steps from the street, I remember to have waited on a lady who had had four children

(I am afraid to write five, though I fully believe it was five) at a birth. This meritorious woman held quite a reception in her room on the morning when I was introduced there, and the sight of the house brought vividly to my mind how the four (five) deceased young people lay, side by side, on a clean cloth on a chest of drawers; reminding me by a homely association, which I suspect their complexion to have assisted, of pigs' feet as they are usually displayed at a neat tripe-shop.

The disturbing similarity between dead pigs and dead babies is echoed by a babbling Mrs Nickleby, a character closely based on Dickens's mother. Having also lost five children in infancy, Mrs Dickens too knew all about dead babies. 'Roast pig', Mrs Nickleby muses:

> 'I hardly think we ever could have had one, now I come to remember, for your papa could never bear the sight of them in the shops, and used to say that they always put him in mind of very little babies, only the pigs had much fairer complexions; and he had a horror of little babies, too, because he couldn't very well afford any increase to his family, and had a natural dislike to the subject. It's very odd now, what can have put that in my head!'

It never left Dickens's head. And it was no joke.

༖ **Dogs** ༖

As his biographer John Forster records, 'Dickens's interest in dogs was inexhaustible'. At Gad's Hill his favoured breeds were Baskerville-big and best avoided. His daughter Mamie recalls:

'Sultan' an Irish bloodhound ... had a bitter experience with his life at Gad's Hill. One evening, having broken his chain, he fell upon a little girl who was passing and bit her so severely that my father considered it necessary to have him shot, although this decision cost him a great deal of sorrow.

Not Mamie, one gathers. There is no 'us' in that last sentence.

Big dogs were his preference but Dickens was nonetheless excessively fond of Mamie's bouncy little Pomeranian, Mrs Bouncer. A leather-and-brass dog collar (unnamed Dickens hound) came up for sale at Bonham's auction in New York in February 2010 and went to some besotted dog-lover (or fanatic Dickensian) for $11,599. It measured 23 inches. It was not, one presumes, Mrs Bouncer's collar.

On his return from his last reading tour in the US, Dickens recorded in a letter the canine welcoming committee of:

The two Newfoundland dogs ['Don' and 'Bumble'] coming to meet me ... lifting their heads to have their ears pulled, – a special attention which they receive from no one else. But when I drove into the stable-yard, Linda (the St Bernard) was greatly excited, weeping profusely, and throwing herself on her back that she might caress my foot with her great fore-paws.

Every dog in Dickens's fiction should be called Fido. In *Oliver Twist*, Bill Sikes's brutalised lethal-weapon mastiff, Bullseye, on witnessing its master accidentally hang himself from a chimney while fleeing the lynch mob, runs

backwards and forwards ... with a dismal howl, and collecting himself for a spring, jumped for the dead man's shoulders.

Missing his aim, he fell into the ditch, turning completely over as he went; and striking his head against a stone, dashed out his brains.

Diogenes, 'a blundering, ill-favoured, clumsy, bullet-headed dog', supplies Florence and Paul Dombey with the love that her father doesn't. In *Barnaby Rudge*, Hugh the Ostler's last request, before he hangs, is that someone look after his dog – the only thing in life that has ever loved him. Dora Copperfield's absurdly pampered lapdog – 'Jip must have a mutton-chop every day at twelve, or he'll die' – does in fact die: not of missing mutton-chops but of grief

Dickens with one of his favourite companions.

for his dead mistress. It is the occasion of what must be one of the most pathetic dog-deaths in literature. Dora dies shortly after childbirth (still birth) and Jip crawls to the bereaved David, and whines to go upstairs.

'Not tonight, Jip! Not tonight!'

He comes very slowly back to me, licks my hand, and lifts his dim eyes to my face.

'Oh, Jip! It may be, never again!'

He lies down at my feet, stretches himself out as if to sleep, and with a plaintive cry, is dead.

One would, to paraphrase Oscar Wilde, need a heart of stone not to bark.

∾ Dust ⌒

Our Mutual Friend is dominated by two metropolitan disgraces: a putrid river, and mephitic 'dustheaps'. What 'dust' means in this context, like 'mud' (*see* 'Street-Sweepings'), is vague. The word has religious connotations ('Dust thou art, and unto dust shalt thou return'). In certain contexts (e.g. 'gold-dust') high value is implied: 'dust' was, in fact, a slang term for 'cash'. But its commonest meaning was the offensive thing that the 'dustman' takes away.

What precisely is in Boffin's mountainous dustheaps? We are given hints in the description of how John Harmon, the great 'dust-contractor', made the fortune Boffin inherits. Harmon:

lived in a hollow in a hilly country entirely composed of Dust. On his own small estate the growling old vagabond threw up his own mountain range, like an old volcano, and its geological formation was Dust. Coal-dust, vegetable-dust, bone-dust, crockery dust, rough dust and sifted dust, – all manner of Dust.

Useful: but what lies within that phrase '*all manner* of Dust'? In 1850 R.H. Horne wrote an essay on the heaps for *Household Words*, Dickens's paper. Entitled 'Dust; or Ugliness Redeemed', it was written in the context of the 1848 'Nuisances Removal and Diseases Prevention Act'.

What 'redeemed' the garbage, Horne argued, was how it was recycled. Ash and cinders were the main constituent. Once sifted out, valuable contents were divided into 'soft-ware' and 'hard-ware'. The former included 'all vegetable and animal matters', destined to be farming manure. Cats were sold (a good catskin could get fourpence, plus another penny for the catgut) to rag and bone shops, like Krook's in *Bleak House*. 'Hard-ware' included 'all broken pottery, pans, crockery, earthenware, oyster-shells, &c., which are sold to make new roads'. Bones were sold off to the soap-maker, rags to the paper-maker, any metal to the scrap yard.

In an otherwise exhaustive survey Horne studiously avoids the delicate question: how much human excrement was in the mix? Controversy was provoked by Humphry House's comment on 'this really sinister question' in *The Dickens World* (1941). The dustheaps, House alleged, contained large amounts of 'decaying human excrement, which was exceedingly valuable as a fertilizer'. It renders scenes such as Silas Wegg puncturing the caked surface of the mounds as he stomps across them with his wooden leg 'almost intolerable'. Put bluntly, the 'Golden Dustman's' gold is his fellow-citizen's shit.

Workers in the dust.

Later critics have argued that the 1848 Act enforced a more sanitary disposal of human faeces than just dumping it in turd mountains by King's Cross. Human waste (designated 'night soil') was collected not by dustmen, who worked by day, but 'nightmen', who disposed of it separately.

The fact is, no one knows. Only a Victorian nose could enlighten us. Or, closely examined, Wegg's peg leg.

ເ⍺ Dwarfs ⍺ว

The most complicated dwarf in Dickens is Miss Mowcher, Steerforth's manicurist, in *David Copperfield*. She is, initially, described with all the callousness of a man for whose age 'freak shows' were a principal entertainment of the people. Miss Mowcher is:

Miss Mowcher.

a pursy dwarf, of about forty or forty-five, with a very large head and face, a pair of roguish grey eyes, and such extremely little arms that to enable herself to lay her finger archly against her snub nose as she ogled Steerforth, she was obliged to meet the finger half-way and lay her nose against it. Her chin, which was what is called a double-chin, was so fat that it entirely swallowed up the strings of her bonnet, bow and all. Throat she had none; waist she had none; legs she had none worth mentioning; for though she was more than full-sized down to where her waist would have been, if she had had any, and though she terminated, as human beings generally do, in a pair of feet, she was so short that she stood at a common-sized chair as at a table, resting a bag she carried on the seat.

Unforgivably, Dickens was describing, with cruel accuracy, a local chiropodist who treated his wife. The little lady complained bitterly. Dickens publicly offered what Michael Slater calls 'the standard novelist's defence' ('any resemblance … coincidental', etc.) but confided to his friend and biographer John Forster: 'there is no doubt one is wrong in being tempted to such a use of power'. His first intention had been to make Mowcher a vicious conspirator with Steerforth in his seductions. He made amends with a nobler Miss Mowcher in the later instalments of *David Copperfield*.

Dickens's powerfully mixed reaction to small people is manifestly sexual. Harry Stone notes, with keen Freudian suspicion, the profusion of 'little women' and 'child wives', as Dora describes herself in *David Copperfield* before going selflessly to her death on the grounds that child wives should not grow old. The list includes (Little) Amy Dorrit, Kate Nickleby, Dolly Varden in *Barnaby Rudge*, Mary Graham in *Martin Chuzzlewit*, and many others in what Stone calls 'the nymph-like host'.

Some nymphs, like Jenny Wren from *Our Mutual Friend*, are as doll-like as the dolls she makes.

Stone argues that 'the most notable real-life counterpart of this angel-seductress was his adored sister-in-law Mary Hogarth, who had died in his arms in 1837 when she was seventeen and he was

Jenny Wren.

twenty-five'. Mrs Dickens, irritatingly, declined to die: something that led to problems at the end of the 1850s.

The sharpest representation of Dickens's complex attitude to little people is in *The Old Curiosity Shop*, where the vile dwarf, Quilp, lusts after the most idealised little woman in Dickens's pages, Little Nell. Both die. Death is a fate far preferable to sex with Daniel Quilp.

ᴄᴏ Elastic Time ᴏᴄ

If there is a hopelessly blunt tool in the kit we have for Victorian fiction, it's that epithet 'Victorian'. What do *Great Expectations* and *Hard Times* have in common? They are novels by Dickens whose action is largely located outside London. What is the great difference separating them? One is set in the pre-Victorian 1820s at the period when the author grew up and when children who stole pork pies (as Pip does) could be transported. The other is set bang in the present, as topical as newspapers reporting the ongoing Preston strike, which the 40-year-old Dickens, in his capacity as a journalist, visited. Ask most students studying *Great Expectations* whether Pip is a Victorian and they will answer 'yes'. He isn't.

The first chore in reading any Dickens novels is to check the calendar. Sometimes he wilfully makes it difficult. *Our Mutual Friend* challenges the reader with its opening proclamation: 'In these times of ours, though concerning the exact year there is no need to be precise …' In few of his novels (*Hard Times* is a notable exception) did Dickens feel the need to be precise. *Little Dorrit*, for example, has the most resonant events in the narrative set in a prison, Marshalsea, long since pulled down. Another key event, that centred on Merdle, alludes to the very recent career and suicide of the swindler John Sadleir, which had just made headlines. In *Nicholas Nickleby* Dickens seems simultaneously to be regarding Yorkshire school ('Dotheboys Hall') scandals of the 1820s and early 1840s. Old and new run through that novel like oil and water.

One useful rule of thumb is to ask how the characters travel. If it's by coach it's the early nineteenth century, before Stevenson's Rocket and the huge railway expansions of the 1830s and 1840s. If by train, it's more likely present-day. But even this can lead to confusion. In *Bleak House*, for example, young Esther travels from Reading to London by stagecoach. Tony Weller from *Pickwick Papers*, we imagine, could be in the driving seat. Many chapters (but only a couple of years) later, Inspector Bucket of the newly formed Scotland Yard travels down to Chesney Wold by express trains. Two time dimensions are in collision here. As Stephen Blackpool of *Hard Times* would say, 'It's aw a muddle'. A very Dickensian muddle. And challenging.

Jolly coaching times.

๛ Englishman's Castle ๛

His 'castle' is what Wemmick in *Great Expectations* calls his home on the Walworth Road. It is, of course, an allusion to the legal proverb, 'An Englishman's home is his castle' (i.e. inviolable without a warrant from higher authority). Wemmick has gone the whole hog on castellation. He also, one notes, keeps a pig in his back-yard, in case his castle comes under siege, he tells Pip.

> Wemmick's house was a little wooden cottage in the midst of plots of garden, and the top of it was cut out and painted like a battery mounted with guns.
>
> 'My own doing,' said Wemmick ...
>
> 'That's a real flagstaff, you see,' said Wemmick, 'and on Sundays I run up a real flag. Then look here. After I have crossed this bridge, I hoist it up – so – and cut off the communication.'
>
> The bridge was a plank, and it crossed a chasm about four feet wide and two deep. But it was very pleasant to see the pride with which he hoisted it up and made it fast; smiling as he did so, with a relish and not merely mechanically.

Dickens mocks the pretensions of British domestic architecture at the time – specifically the effect of the art critic John Ruskin's writings. The sage lived just up the road from Wemmick, on salubrious Denmark Hill. He had, said Ruskin looking down that hill, brought Venice to Camberwell. He was not proud of the achievement.

There is a smack of Wemmick the castle-owner in Dickens himself. He records it, with touching self-mockery, in a late 'Uncommercial Traveller' essay of 1860. On the road just outside Chatham, the traveller meets 'a very queer small boy', nine years old, it emerges. He is looking intently through the railings at a large house:

'You admire that house?' said I.

'Bless you, sir,' said the very queer small boy, 'when I was not more than half as old as nine, it used to be a treat for me to be brought to look at it. And now I am nine, I come by myself to look at it. And ever since I can recollect, my father, seeing me so fond of it, has often said to me, "If you were to be very persevering and were to work hard, you might some day come to live in it." Though that's impossible!' said the very queer small boy, drawing a low breath, and now staring at the house out of window [*sic*] with all his might.

The queer little boy is Charles Dickens. It was, as it happened, very possible. The house is Gad's Hill Place. Dickens bought it in 1856, and lived in it from 1860. He died there.

Gad's Hill.

ᘒ **Fagins** ᘒ

The Jewish fence who gives Oliver refuge in his thieves' kitchen is the most argued-over figure in Dickens's fiction. My own first awareness of Dickens (at around Pip's age) was seeing the David Lean film of *Oliver Twist* in 1948, in Colchester's Hippodrome cinema.

Alec Guinness's Fagin gave little John Sutherland nightmares. It was also, in the context of the concentration camps, widely regarded as anti-Semitic. Even at the time of publication Dickens received protests from his readers, and in later reprints he tinkered with the text to make it marginally less offensive. He is assumed to have created the money-lender Riah, in *Our Mutual Friend*, as a more substantial apologetic gesture. Dickens was not, it is generally agreed, as anti-Semitic (in the tolerated Victorian way) as Thackeray or Trollope, and not as philo-Semitic as George Eliot or Disraeli.

Fagin is an ambiguous figure. He is the first person in the novel to show kindness to Oliver. Were it not for 'the Jew' the hero would have starved. But what are Fagin's motives in taking the young stranger into his pickpockets' academy? There were children enough roaming the streets, most of them as light-fingered, most of them less morally scrupulous. The wholly improbable Monks plot involving the family and inheritance relationship between hero and villain has not yet been worked into the narrative (because Dickens had not yet thought of it, one presumes).

Is the 'merry old gentleman', as the traditional phrase suggests, 'diabolic'? Is he, even worse, a pederast? Those 'my dears' make the skin creep. So too does the way Fagin treats his newly arrived recruit. After Oliver has eaten the first good meal, probably, he has had in his life:

> [T]he Jew then mixed him a glass of hot gin-and-water: telling
> him he must drink it off directly, because another gentleman
> wanted the tumbler. Oliver did as he was desired. Immediately
> afterwards he felt himself gently lifted on to one of the sacks;
> and then he sunk into a deep sleep.

Is the drink drugged? Is Oliver abused in his sleep? Such things
happen.

Fagin's name is another curiosity. It's Irish-sounding. If he
was going to be anti-Semitic, why did Dickens not come up with
something more like 'Ikey Solomon', the fence on whom Fagin
was historically based? It's further complicated by the so-called
autobiographical fragment (*see* 'Fragments'). The only person to
show kindness to young Charles Dickens when he was put to work
in Warren's blacking factory was, Dickens recalled, 'Bob Fagin'. A
'much older and bigger' boy, 'in a ragged apron and a paper cap',
Bob instructed Charles how to wrap the blacking bottles and
protected him from other young louts who bullied him for being
'a little gentleman'.

Most interestingly, as Dickens recalls:

> Bob Fagin was very good to me on the occasion of a bad attack
> of my old disorder [spasms in the side]. I suffered such excruci-
> ating pain that time, that they made a temporary bed of straw in
> my old recess in the counting-house, and I rolled about on the
> floor, and Bob filled empty blacking-bottles with hot water, and
> applied relays of them to my side.

As Dickens comments, without explanation, 'I took the liberty of
using his name, long afterwards, in *Oliver Twist*'. Critics have been
only too willing to supply the explanation. It was 'a friendship',

asserts the Freudian critic Steven Marcus, 'that is both needed and intolerable', replaying, as it did, 'the fantasy of the primal parental coitus'.

It will be a theory too far for many readers, but there remains something very strange about the two Fagins.

ᴄ∂ Farewells ᴔ∾

There is a startlingly high mortality rate in Dickens's fiction. Few companies would insure the lives of his dramatis personae. A quiz. Whose are the following last words?

1. 'Willin''
2. 'Whosoever liveth and believeth in me shall never die'
3. 'Faster, faster!'
4. 'Hallowed – be – thy'
5. 'dear boy'
6. 'Will somebody be pleased to cover my face'
7. 'It is much better as it is'
8. 'The light about the head is shining on me as I go!'
9. 'I am so sad – so very, very sad'
10. 'On the ground'

1. Barkis is willin' – he goes out with the tide, as foretold, at three o'clock in the morning (in *David Copperfield*). Dickens was fascinated by how killingly bleak the world seemed at this lowest point of the circadian cycle.

2. It is commonly misbelieved that Darnay's last word in *A Tale of Two Cities*, before Madame Guillotine chops off his head, is: 'It is

a far, far better thing that I do, than I have ever done', etc. In fact he does not say this; it's not clear that he even thinks it – it's what he *might* have said.

3. Fagin's last words in *Oliver Twist* – he is deluded into thinking not that he is going to the gallows, to be publicly hanged, but that Oliver is somehow contriving to smuggle him out. Oliver stays on to watch the execution.

4. Jo's last words, with the prayer incomplete, in *Bleak House*. It's the first time the little street-sweeper has encountered it. He thinks it 'wery good'. Being able to recite the Lord's Prayer was a test to ensure that illiterate children like Jo were fit to give evidence in court.

5. Magwitch's last words from *Great Expectations*: 'I don't complain of none [i.e. pain] dear boy.' He is lying on his condemned man's bed. His last communication is to press Pip's hand, on being told of his daughter, Estella.

6. Stephen Blackpool's last utterance, after his shattered body is lifted out of Hell Hole Shaft in *Hard Times*. Dickens wrote 'soombody' and 'coover' – his ear, so sound on cockney, is unimpressive on the Lancashire accent.

7. Dora's last words – consigning David Copperfield to the care of Agnes. She, Dora, is a child wife and could never have grown old.

8. Paul Dombey's last words. The light is from a vision of his dead, haloed mother.

9. Little Nell's last words (from *The Old Curiosity Shop*). None sadder, whatever the scoffers say about needing a heart of stone not to laugh.

10. Dickens's own last words, before his stroke rendered him wordless. It is strange that he did not assent, as his sister-in-law Georgina urged, to be put on the couch.

ᥩ **Fat Boy** ᥩ

In an earlier entry (*see* 'Children') it was alleged that there was no child in the first novel Dickens conceived, *Barnaby Rudge*, nor in the first he published, *The Pickwick Papers*. It's not quite true, and interestingly not true. There is one prominent child, but not of the kind (angelic, impish, orphan, waifish) that one normally associates with Dickens. It is, of course, the fat boy in *Pickwick*.

One should note (as a word search on the e-text will ascertain) that there are a lot of fat characters in this jolliest of Dickens's novels – including the pot-bellied hero. No Dickensian dramatis personae displays more obesity. If one could apply a BMI to Dickens's fiction, his first is well over the 30 mark.

There is, however, nothing jolly about the fat boy's corpulence. Jollity is active. Active this young fellow is not, even though he is one of Dickens's under-aged workers, the driver's assistant on the stagecoach. The fat boy could be overtaken by the average snail on a slow crawl day. It's his job to help passengers in and out of the vehicle and look after the refreshments (which he sleepily, but constantly raids). His features suggest a pathological condition – as, for example, when he may, or may not, have been eavesdropping on Mr Tupman doing something rather secretive in the bushes:

> Mr Tupman looked round. There was the fat boy, perfectly motionless, with his large circular eyes staring into the arbour, but without the slightest expression on his face that the most expert

physiognomist could have referred to astonishment, curiosity, or any other known passion that agitates the human breast.

The world had to wait 120 years until, in 1956, C.S. Burwell, an expert clinician and not a physiognomist, diagnosed the symptoms that Dickens so accurately reports. The fat boy is suffering from obesity hypoventilation syndrome. Burwell went on to name it 'Pickwickian syndrome', under which it will be found in all the medical textbooks.

The fat boy.

✺ Fishers of Men ✺

The novelist John Irving is on record as saying that he was hold-ing *Our Mutual Friend* back for his deathbed read. Desmond in the cult TV series *Lost* said the same thing. It's a wise decision not to rush at Dickens's last completed novel. It was written late and, ideally, should be confronted late. Late, that is, in one's reading of the author's works and late in one's own life – at that point where the grim reaper's rap on the door will be no great surprise.

If, 60 years ago, you'd asked me what my favourite Dickens work was, I would have replied (having been glued, eye-poppingly, to my seat by the David Lean movie), '*Oliver Twist*'. In my middle years, it would have been a toss-up between *Dombey and Son* and *Bleak House*. Now (is that a knock on the door I hear?) it's – you've guessed it.

'Strike the Keynote!', Dickens liked to tell himself in the terse working notes he drew up for his novels in progress (*see* 'Keynotes'). The opening sentence of *Our Mutual Friend* strikes that keynote with a dark and hard hand:

> In these times of ours, though concerning the exact year there is no need to be precise, a boat of dirty and disreputable appear-ance, with two figures in it, floated on the Thames, between Southwark bridge which is of iron, and London Bridge which is of stone, as an autumn evening was closing in.

Dickens instructed his artist, Marcus Stone, to accompany the scene with a keynote illustration, entitled 'Bird of Prey'. The man, one observes, has caught something – but what is it precisely? A corpse, it transpires. 'I will make you fishers of men', our Saviour said. He did not mean it in the sense that Gaffer Hexam fishes for his fellow kind (suicides, in the main) out of that filthy river, whose 'big stinks' in summer would bring the whole city to a standstill.

'Bird of Prey'.

Our Mutual Friend is haunted by death and God's grim curse: 'Dust thou art, and unto dust shalt thou return' (*see* 'Dust'). Dickens himself, during its composition, was lucky to escape being killed (as scores of his fellow passengers were) in the terrible Staplehurst train accident on 9 June 1865 (*see* 'Staplehurst'). He, like Hexam in his boat, had a young girl in attendance on that fateful trip – his mistress, Ellen ('Nelly') Ternan.

The Victorians loved Dickens, but they did not entirely love *Our Mutual Friend*. Henry James spoke for many when he called it 'the poorest of Mr Dickens's works'. Why didn't his contemporaries like it? Because, as does much great literature, *Our Mutual Friend* disturbs us to the root of our being. Who, hand on heart, 'likes' *King Lear*? But who would deny that it's the greatest play in the Shakespearean canon?

Henry James was a mere 25 years old when he penned that derogatory judgement on *Our Mutual Friend*. One would like to think that, 40 years on, he came to see it for what it is. Terrible, yes. But terribly great. Read *Our Mutual Friend*. But not unless you are entirely confident you are ready for it.

⸂⁄⁄⁄⸃ Fog ⸂⁄⁄⁄⸃

Victorian air was different from ours. It was purer in the country, filthier in town. They also had a different theory about what it was they were gulping into their lungs. Victorians held to the miasmic, not the contagious, theory of disease. Rural and seaside air was curative; city air was bad (*malaria*, the Italians called it).

The bigger the city, the badder the air. No city was bigger than London. If you could have put it in packets, like today's cigarettes, London air should have carried the inscription 'Air Kills' (Victorians believed, perversely, that their gaspers were medicinal).

As hundreds of thousands of student essays parrot every year, taking their cue from the magnificent 'Fog everywhere …' rhapsody, the fog in *Bleak House* 'symbolises' the connectedness underlying the stupendous fragmentariness of London. So it does. But it was also real for the Victorian Londoner inhaling it in ways that it can never be for us. For them it wasn't a literary device but airborne excrement. First readers of the first chapter of *Bleak House* in March 1852 would have responded with their lungs as much as with their eyes.

The first reference to aerial filth is not fog but, significantly, 'Smoke lowering down from chimney-pots, making a soft black drizzle, with flakes of soot in it as big as full-grown snowflakes'. Combine that soot with the damp air blowing into the city from the marshes in Kent and you have a lethal cocktail – airborne sulphuric acid, distilled from a million coal fires, trapped by inversion and brewed into maximum toxicity. It looked as bad as it tasted. As one commentator put it in 1855: 'Sometimes it is of a bottle-green colour, but at other times it is a pea-soup yellow.'

An impressionist painter such as Monet could see a visual beauty in London fog but for most it meant inflamed lungs, gobby phlegm and – at its worst – death by chronic suffocation. Dickens, one may note, was a lifelong martyr to head colds and nasal congestion. A 'foggy day in London town' really could get him down.

The 'London particulars' or 'pea soupers' disappeared from the metropolis in 1953 after a particularly horrible November in which thousands died. The Clean Air Act passed through Parliament at panic speed. Thereafter it was, in Dickensian terms, 'Fog nowhere'.

৬৯ Fragments ৫৩

Dickens was ruthless in his campaign against what Henry James called 'the post-mortem exploiter' – the biographers, that is, who would rake over his life after he was gone. Dickens set out to foil these lice on the locks of literature by destroying every letter and private paper in his possession (*see* 'Onions').

At the astonishingly premature age of 37, he appointed his bosom friend, John Forster, as his biographer. And it was to Forster he entrusted the unpublished 'autobiographical fragment' – that short sketch of his childhood which, like a plutonium pellet, has irradiated every biography since.

The effect of the fragment was to cast Dickens for ever as the kind of innocent martyrised child elsewhere rendered talismanic in his fiction. The fragment relates two traumatising events: his father's incarceration in the Marshalsea debtors' prison; and his own 'agony of soul' at being sent for a few months to work in a boot-blacking-fluid factory by the Thames, to assist the family's dire finances. Both events are dramatised less in terms of the Dickens family tribulation than as culpable cruelty towards little Charles.

The whole family, less Charles, kept John Dickens company in the prison. Charles made visits that were exquisite torment to him. Marshalsea was also where those accused of 'unnatural crimes' were held. The pretty twelve-year-old boy would probably have been ogled.

Worse was the blacking factory. His family sent him there, he bitterly recalls, as happily as if he was being sent off to Cambridge University. For the whole of his life he would make huge detours to avoid Hungerford Stairs where that awful Warren's factory had once been.

There is no confirmation of the details of these juvenile traumas other than Dickens's own confidential memorandum to Forster. Why did Dickens confide these life-changingly shameful events to Forster alone, along with the commission to write up his life? The motive was not confession, one suspects, but image control. The 'Great Inimitable' intended to fix his image, unchangeably, for posterity. He was, through Forster, 'writing himself'.

Forster moulded the Dickensian image as instructed, using the 'fragment' as his foundation stone and his Rosetta Stone – the key to understanding this great man. The fragment, and its traumatic narrative, was central to the biography, produced only months after Dickens's death. Forster had also been given large caches of correspondence and private papers by Dickens, who did not, manifestly, burn everything in 1860. Forster duly did go on to destroy much of it – having incorporated what he needed.

We have, and always shall have, unchangeable in all its essentials, the mummified image of Dickens that Dickens cunningly, through his cat's-paw biographer, erected for us. Subsequent biographers can throw new light at the auto-icon, but they cannot change what is there. Dickens made sure of that.

୭ Gamp ୭

Of all the nurses a sick person would not want to have attend on them, the most unpleasant is Mrs 'Sairey' Gamp, in *Martin Chuzzlewit*. We meet the lady in Chapter 19 where she is given the full Dickensian-descriptive treatment:

> She was a fat old woman, this Mrs Gamp, with a husky voice and a moist eye, which she had a remarkable power of turning up, and only showing the white of it. ... The face of Mrs Gamp – the nose in particular – was somewhat red and swollen, and it was difficult to enjoy her society without becoming conscious of a smell of spirits. Like most persons who have attained to great eminence in their profession, she took to hers very kindly; insomuch that, setting aside her natural predilections as a woman, she went to a lying-in or a laying-out with equal zest and relish.
>
> 'Ah!' repeated Mrs Gamp; for it was always a safe sentiment in cases of mourning. 'Ah dear! When Gamp was summoned to his long home, and I see him a-lying in Guy's Hospital with a penny-piece on each eye, and his wooden leg under his left arm, I thought I should have fainted away. But I bore up.'

Gin helps.

Mrs Gamp with her 'gamp'.

Her name lives (few of her patients do) and has become folkloric; it is also the metonym – i.e. a part signifying a whole – for, as the *OED* tells us: '1. a monthly nurse or sick nurse of a disreputable class. 2. a very large, bulgy, loosely tied cotton umbrella.' More specifically Mrs Gamp's umbrella is a 'gig umbrella … in colour like a faded leaf, except where a circular patch of a lively blue had been dexterously let in at the top'.

Dickens knew all about nurses. In October 1841, a few months before beginning the composition of *Chuzzlewit*, he had a fistula removed from his anus – without anaesthetic. A short-term (i.e. monthly) nurse would have been required after the operation. The notion of some Mrs Gamp dressing his wound must have made him writhe even more than did the surgeon's knife.

It is an oddity that the word 'umbrella' is mentioned 55 times in *Martin Chuzzlewit* – most of the characters are described carrying one. Most Dickens novels are umbrella-less. There is a good reason for their presence in this one novel. Dickens began thinking about *Chuzzlewit* in 1841. It was the wettest year in the UK, with 895mm precipitation, since records began in 1767. There have been only two wetter (1903, 1960) since.

✇ Gruel ✇

Gruel is not an item much found on menus nowadays. The word is familiar enough. Victorians, on whose menu it often featured, knew precisely what gruel was and what it tasted like. Thin porridge – oatmeal soaked in water (or milk if you were very lucky) then heated and served as a soup.

Gruel was much favoured in schools, hospitals, and workhouses. It was cheap and could be prepared easily in a large copper to be ladled out by one person. It required no cooking skills.

Dickens goes into detail about gruel in the second chapter of *Oliver Twist*. The managing board of the Mudfog workhouse love the stuff. They love serving it out to the unfortunates in their charge, that is.

> The members of this board were very sage, deep, philosophical men … So, they established the rule, that all poor people should have the alternative (for they would compel nobody, not

they), of being starved by a gradual process in the house, or by a quick one out of it. With this view, they contracted with the water-works to lay on an unlimited supply of water; and with a corn-factor to supply periodically small quantities of oatmeal; and issued three meals of thin gruel a day, with an onion twice a week, and half a roll on Sundays.

So close do Oliver and his companions come to starving on their gruel diet that they resolve, if the ration is not increased, to resort to cannibalism. A 'weakly youth of tender age' has already been selected (*see* 'Cannibalism').

George Cruikshank

Oliver wants more gruel.

One of the advantages of gruel was that it could readily be strengthened, by boards more humane than Mudfog's, with whatever protein was going. The fortification might not always be something you'd want to know about. In the inquest scene in *Bleak House*, juvenile onlookers taunt the beadles with catcalls about a 'boy being made into soup for the workhouse'. The allusion is to a street ballad, 'The Poor Workhouse Boy'. The final verse runs:

> At length the soup copper repairs did need,
> The Coppersmith came, and there he seed,
> A dollop of bones lay a grizzling there,
> In the leg of the breeches the poor boy did vear!
> To gain his fill the boy did stoop,
> And, dreadful to tell, he was boil'd in the soup!

Please sir, no more.

↪ Hands ↩

Every Dickens novel has a master image. In *Our Mutual Friend* it is the river. In *Bleak House* it is the fog. In *Little Dorrit* it is the prison. In *Great Expectations* it is the hand. We often know much more about the principals' hands in that novel than their faces. Who, when the name Magwitch is mentioned, does not think of those murderous 'large brown veinous hands'? Jaggers? One's nose twitches – scented soap (the lawyer, like Pontius Pilate, is forever washing his hands). Miss Havisham? Withered claws. So it goes.

Pip is brought up 'by hand'. The fact is drummed into him ad nauseam by Mrs Joe and Pumblechook. Primarily it means that when his mother died delivering him into the world Mrs Joe vindictively took on the chore of feeding him by hand (i.e. bottle). Her hand, as he grows up, is transferred to the task of cuffing, slapping and throwing him against the wall so hard the whitewash sticks to his skin like talcum powder.

Pip's destiny as 'the blacksmith's boy' is to be a 'manual', i.e. a hand worker not a brain worker (Victorians drew a strict division between the two). After his experiences at Satis House, Pip becomes pathologically ashamed of his 'black hands'. He wants to be a gentleman, he tells Biddy (whose hands are not, he notices, exceptionally clean). His great expectations include white gloves and a soft white epidermis inside them. Those expectations collapse and his hands are, literally, burned almost to the bone in the great Satis House fire.

Critics have gone on to note strangely erotic aspects to the hand image in *Great Expectations*. When Magwitch returns from Australia, to Pip's horror the first thing he does is slobberingly kiss Pip's gentlemanly hands – he, Magwitch, has, of course, made them kissable.

The most adventurous exploration of this eroto-manual theme is by William A. Cohen who reads the novel as a 'masturbator's manual', with close attention to such moments as Pip stuffing his bread and butter into his trouser groin (intending to smuggle it later to his convict, Magwitch, in the marshes). The yellow butter oozes down his leg. Drawing on such imagery, Cohen sees the early chapters as suffused with what could coarsely be called wanker's guilt. 'Like many avid masturbators', he informs us, 'Pip is deeply ashamed, and just short of growing hair on his palms, he transfers his generalized guilt onto his hands themselves.'

What is it Lady Macbeth says? 'Will this little hand ne'er be clean?' No, nor, if we follow Professor Cohen, will Pip's naughty little hand.

ᩔ **Hanged Man** ᩕ

Dickens witnessed hangings, we know (*see* 'Courvoisier') but he also saw 'hanged men': that is, corpses left to rot after death, as a warning to other potential criminals.

In *Great Expectations*, little Pip, after his blood-curdling encounter with Magwitch on the marshes, makes his way home, a very troubled child. He is, he now knows, born to hang: something his sister has often told him. He lifts his eyes and sees on the horizon 'a gibbet, with some chains hanging to it, which had once contained a pirate'.

There is, we recall (Dickens certainly did) a similarly-viewed gibbet in Wordsworth's autobiographical poem *The Prelude*. Still an 'urchin' (five years old, a year younger than Pip), the future poet lost his way in the hills and

> Came to a bottom, where in former times
> A murderer had been hung in iron chains.
> The gibbet-mast had mouldered down, the bones
> And iron case were gone; but on the turf,
> Hard by, soon after that fell deed was wrought,
> Some unknown hand had carved the murderer's name.

In the countryside the apparatus was used so that the body could not be taken down and given a Christian burial by the family (the 'Murder Act' of 1751 forbade that). This is the famous 'spots of time' moment in Wordsworth's poem when he, like Pip, first became aware of 'the identity of things'.

Alongside sea-route estuaries gibbeted men (captured pirates or mutineers, typically) were left in cages to rot, to remind sailors to behave well. There was, research suggests, no gibbet on the

Cliffe marshes, where the scene with Magwitch is set. Dickens was thinking of one that was alongside the Medway, by Chatham dockyard. He would, when Pip's age, have seen it many times. His father worked nearby in the Navy pay office.

Men were still being gibbeted along the Kent coast until 1830. That the barbarism stuck, nightmarishly, in Dickens's mind is borne out by the description of the death of Gaspard in *A Tale of Two Cities*. After his execution for the murder of 'Monseigneur', his mutilated corpse is left hanging and drips blood in a gallows, 40 feet over the village fountain, poisoning the water until his body shrivels and dries out into a husk. These, the novel argues, are the kinds of things that inspire revolution.

৵ Hanged Turkey ৶

The second most famous scene in Dickens (no need to say what the first is – think gruel and workhouses) is the regenerate Scrooge leaning out of his window on a sunny Christmas Day. He hails a boy in the street and asks:

> 'Do you know whether they've sold the prize Turkey that was hanging up there? – Not the little prize Turkey: the big one?'
>
> 'What, the one as big as me?' returned the boy.
>
> 'What a delightful boy!' said Scrooge. 'It's a pleasure to talk to him. Yes, my buck!'
>
> 'It's hanging there now,' replied the boy.
>
> 'Is it?' said Scrooge. 'Go and buy it.'

It will be sent, of course, to the Cratchit household as a mystery Christmas present.

Turkeys were highly valued by Victorians for two reasons. The meat was white and dry, unlike dark and greasy goose, swan, or duck. And there was enough on a big turkey for a big family all to dine on the same bird (like the fatted calf). It added to the festive sense of community.

The practice of turkey at Christmas was long established. They were driven from as far afield as Norfolk for the London market. Turkeys walk briskly enough, but keeping them flocked together was tricky. Dogs and drovers with sticks were used (the sticks would have red flags on them – more even than bulls, turkeys hated that colour). It was one of the sights of Christmas.

One should attend to Scrooge's repeated word 'hanging'. It's always loaded in Dickens's fiction. Turkey meat was prized for its whiteness. Cruelty was required to get that valued hue. William Howitt, in *The Rural Life of England* (1838), describes how it was done. He was staying with a 'delicate lady', and

> passing the kitchen door at ten in the morning, saw a turkey suspended by its heels, and bleeding from its bill, drop by drop. Supposing it was just in its last struggles from a recent death-wound, I passed on … On accidentally passing by the same kitchen door in the afternoon, six hours afterwards, I beheld, to my astonishment, the same turkey suspended from the same nail, still bleeding, drop by drop, and still giving an occasional flutter with its wings! Hastening to the kitchen, I inquired of the cook, if she knew that the turkey was not dead. 'Yes, sir,' she replied, 'it won't be dead, may-happen, these two hours. We always kill turkeys that way, it so improves their colour; they have a vein opened under the tongue, and only bleed a drop at a time.'

Bon appetit, Cratchits.

৶ Hearts ৶

If you boiled Dickens's thinking about politics down until only one thing remained, observed Humphry House, that one thing would be a sugar lump called 'benevolence'.

The world, as Dickens saw it, was full of hard hearts. How to soften them? If one lets fancy run riot, three ghosts making their ghostly points about time past, present and future will do it, as with Scrooge. But that, alas, happens only in fairy stories.

The 'change of heart' is a crucial moment in Dickens's big novels. There it's a much more complex thing than Scrooge leaning out of his window and ordering turkeys for the poor until he is himself impoverished by his rash benevolence. As portrayed in Dickens's fiction, cardiac reform is more painful than a heart transplant without anaesthetic.

Mr Dombey, for example, has to lose the thing that mattered more to him, almost, than life itself (certainly his son's life): 'the Firm of Dombey and Son: Wholesale, Retail and for Exportation'. In *Hard Times*, Gradgrind's heart is not softened until he sees his daughter lying at his feet, that most horrible thing to a respectable Victorian paterfamilias, a whore. 'Father', she tells him, 'you have brought me to this':

> He tightened his hold in time to prevent her sinking on the floor, but she cried out in a terrible voice, 'I shall die if you hold me! Let me fall upon the ground!' And he laid her down there, and saw the pride of his heart and the triumph of his system, lying, an insensible heap, at his feet.

His hair turns white in a few weeks. But his heart softens, instantly.

Eugene Wrayburn, in *Our Mutual Friend*, requires a morally therapeutic skull fracture (helpfully inflicted by Bradley Headstone) to bring about the same result. The most grisly change of heart in Dickens is, however, that of Mrs Joe in *Great Expectations*. The competition for the 'hardest-hearted woman' award in his fiction would be fierce – Miss Havisham and Estella, and Mrs Clennam from *Little Dorrit*, would all be in contention. But Mrs Joe would win – until, that is, her heart is changed.

Eugene on the way to recovery.

What brings it about? Orlick creeps up behind her and clubs her on the head even more savagely than Headstone does Wrayburn. Mrs Joe survives a vegetable – but a good-hearted vegetable. Capable only of mumbling, dribbling and scrawling on a slate, she is excessively obsequious to Orlick (who escapes punishment). And her last, inarticulate request is that Joe and Pip forgive her.

One is reminded of Swift's 'Last week I saw a woman flayed and you will hardly believe how much it altered her person for the worse'. But perhaps it softened her heart?

✐ Home for the Homeless ✐

In 1859 it was estimated that there were 55,000 whores in London. Many of them were 'streetwalkers' – women without a home. 'Castaways', 'the Fallen', 'Magdalens' were favoured euphemisms for these human discards.

Claire Tomalin, in the novelist's latest biography, claims, plausibly, that 'it is not impossible to believe' that a ferociously sexual man like Dickens used prostitutes. 'Mrs Dickens is in a very uninteresting condition', he would complain to friends. What then did he do in her virtually continual pregnancy during the years of their marital cohabitation? Their last child, of ten, was born in 1852. She was still in her thirties, and pre-menopausal for years more. One presumes, from the births register, that sexual relations between them had stopped. Had all sexual relations stopped for him?

If he did use prostitutes, Dickens repaid the profession handsomely. As the reformer William Acton observed, 'to attempt to put down prostitution by law is to attempt the impossible'.

But something had to be done about a contingent of fallen women larger than the British Army and Navy combined (both bodies, of course, reliable users of prostitutes). Dickens, more successfully than any official body, took on the challenge of getting unfortunate (but worthy) women off the street.

In 1846 he set up a reformatory, supported financially by Angela Burdett-Coutts, the second-wealthiest woman in England – but wholly unknowledgeable about her fallen sisters. It was known as Urania Cottage (so called by a previous owner). 'Urania' elicits a chortle in many modern readers, who associate it with the planet Uranus and lame schoolboy puns. Urania was, mythologically, one of the nine muses: a pure woman. They continued (somewhat inappropriately) to call it a 'cottage' to distinguish it from penitentiaries. Dark satanic mills, all of them.

Dickens managed the Home for the Homeless (as it was misleadingly advertised) for eleven years. There were two superintendents and thirteen inmates at any one time. They were recruited from prisons, courts, and workhouses. Entrants were selected after a one-on-one interview (by Dickens) to ascertain a basic 'good character' – the 'pure drop of water at the bottom of the weed-choked well', as he elsewhere called it.

Dickens decreed no preaching (he fired a superintendent who proved too evangelical), no garish dress (but no uniform), and instruction in basic literacy, useful domestic skills, and personal hygiene. Reformed graduates were given assisted passage to the colonies where, disguising their past (desperately hoping, presumably, they did not encounter previous clients), they could make good marriages and live decent lives.

After the cottage had been running five years 57 girls had made it to graduation. Thirty had gone on to make futures for themselves in the colonies, principally Australia. 'Wives is very scarce theer',

Peggotty tells David Copperfield. Seven found husbands in Britain. The remainder fell by the wayside. It made no dent on 55,000 but it was a noble achievement and one admires Dickens for it.

Dickens left Urania Cottage in 1858 when he fell out with Miss Burdett-Coutts over his mistress Ellen Ternan. As Philip Collins tartly notes:

> It is one of the ironies of Dickens's life that his connection with Urania Cottage ceased through his involvement in an affair which might have qualified yet another girl for entry into a Home for Fallen Women.

Gentlemen are discreet about their intercourse with whores. Dickens never allowed it to be publicly known that he was connected with Urania Cottage.

ఞ Horseman ఞ

How would the reader of *Dombey and Son* instantly know that Mr Carker, a toothy man on a horse, is a double-died villain?

In Dickens's fiction only swine ride horses. How does Bentley Drummle (wife-beater) die? It's chronicled in the 'suppressed ending' of *Great Expectations*: 'I had heard of the death of her husband, from an accident consequent on his ill-treatment of a horse.' (Dickens dropped this much less upbeat ending in which Pip and Estella are not united – wrongly as many readers will think – on the advice of a friend, and came up with the cheerful conclusion we have in the printed text.)

Horses are everywhere in Dickens's world and in his fictional world, and Bentley's death (good thing too!) is as common as a traffic death today. Victorian society ran on two great power sources: two-legged servants and four-legged servants.

Dickens is often compared to Robert Surtees, whose Jorrocks (cockney grocer turned squire and horseman) clearly owes everything to Pickwick. Surtees's first publication was not a novel, but *The Horseman's Manual*. As illustrated (sublimely) by John Leech, Surtees's novels are dominated by hunting scenes and characters on horseback.

Horses are beasts you ride in Surtees, as they are in Trollope ('the novelist who hunted the fox', as Henry James acidly called him). The Marxist critic, Georg Lukács, instructed that we should always look for the 'invisible serf' in the fiction of Tolstoy – that anonymous army who make the Tolstoyan world go round. Two-legged servants are very visible in Dickens's world (e.g. Sam Weller in *Pickwick*, Mark Tapley in *Chuzzlewit*). But among his horses not one, as I recall, has a name or a personality (many do in Surtees).

In Dickens's narratives the horses are typically draught animals. One thinks of Barkis and his cart in *David Copperfield*; the Dover mail on the muddy road in *A Tale of Two Cities*, and later the obnoxious 'Monseigneur in his Coach'. When Pip makes his trips to and from London in *Great Expectations* it is always via The Blue Boar coaching inn. So too when Mr Pickwick makes his epic journey to The Angel at Bury St Edmunds (a still-existent former coaching inn that has canonised the gentleman to the level of St Edmund himself).

When Dickens made neurotic night-time trips to Rochester, he walked (*see* 'Perambulation'). He could have ridden. Most Victorian gentlemen as well set up as Dickens would have had their groom fetch a beast from the mews stable and galloped off down the Old Kent Road, not foot-slogged it like some peasant.

From childhood onwards, it had been ground into Charles that he was not one of the horse-riding class. John Dickens's father could never afford a stable or tackle – it was like being below the salt, outside the pale, or, Pip's disgusted epithet for himself, 'common'.

It's not difficult to reconstruct the psychology by which characters in the saddle are almost always villains like Carker and Drummle. Dickens loved some animals (*see* 'Dogs' and 'Ravens'). Some he hated (*see* 'Rats' and 'Cats'). Horses he seems neither to have loved nor hated. But he had prejudices about them. Social prejudices. And however rich and famous he became, he never outgrew them.

⟡ Hue and Cry ⟡

Dickens was never sure whether he liked modern systems of justice, or the old-fashioned ways. There is, in his jurisprudential make-up, a mixture of prison reformer Elizabeth Fry and 'hanging' Judge Jeffreys.

One thing is clear. The old-fashioned ways excited his imagination more than criminal reform did. Reading Dickens one is reminded of President George W. Bush, in the crisis of 9/11, deciding it was time ('Wanted: dead or alive') to go back to the simplicities of the Wild West.

What, before Peel's police and penalty reforms, could law-abiding citizens do, if they witnessed a crime in progress? There were no 999/911 calls available, or patrolling 'bobbies' (named, of course, after Robert Peel), or sheriffs. The only citizens' resource was to form an ad hoc *posse comitatus* and give chase. This was the so-called 'hue and cry'.

There are two hue and cry scenes in *Oliver Twist*. The first is the more thoughtful. Brownlow browses at the outside shelf of a bookstore. Oliver watches as Artful Dodger 'dips' – picks the gent's pocket. Suddenly Oliver understands what the future holds for him if he sticks with Fagin. It's from that destiny that he makes the fateful decision to run for it. A hue and cry is raised. It's vividly described. Dickens then stops his narrative for a minute to ponder what he has just been describing:

'Stop thief! Stop thief!' There is a magic in the sound. The tradesman leaves his counter, and the car-man his waggon; the butcher throws down his tray; the baker his basket; the milkman his pail; the errand-boy his parcels; the school-boy his marbles; the paviour his pickaxe; the child his battledore. Away they run, pell-mell, helter-skelter, slap-dash: tearing, yelling, screaming, knocking down the passengers as they turn the corners, rousing up the dogs, and astonishing the fowls: and streets, squares, and courts, re-echo with the sound.

'Stop thief! Stop thief!' The cry is taken up by a hundred voices, and the crowd accumulate at every turning. Away they fly, splashing through the mud, and rattling along the pavements: up go the windows, out run the people, onward bear the mob, a whole audience desert Punch in the very thickest of the plot, and, joining the rushing throng, swell the shout, and lend fresh vigour to the cry, 'Stop thief! Stop thief!'

'Stop thief! Stop thief!' There is a passion for hunting something deeply implanted in the human breast.

Not least, as he candidly intimates, in Boz's breast.

～ Incest ～

Few great writers have been accused of incest, the most unpleasant of domestic crimes. Some (notably Virginia Woolf) have been
victims of it. The suspicion, however, has always hovered around
Dickens.

Dickens was brought up with numerous females in the family
household. In his adult life he always needed a harem of women
('petticoats', as he called them) in the many homes he set up. When
he married, he brought his sixteen-year-old sister-in-law, Mary
Hogarth, into his house. When, still a girl, she collapsed and suddenly died, he held her in his arms as she passed away and took
from her still warm finger a ring that he wore on his own hand
until he died – a symbolic marriage of longer duration than that
solemnised in church with her elder sister. He kept Mary's clothes
all his life – Miss Havisham originates in that fact.

Mary's death was so traumatic that, for the only time in his
career, he stopped writing. But, as Claire Tomalin notes:

> It is curious that during the fourteen hours between her col-
> lapse and death no doctor was able to make any diagnosis, or to
> provide or even suggest any form of care or treatment beyond
> allowing Dickens to administer brandy and hold the sick girl in
> his arms.

Was he, like Michael Jackson's doctor, guilty of culpable
manslaughter?

The incest suspicion cropped up again when Dickens separated
from his wife, establishing another sister, Georgina Hogarth, as
his housekeeper (his daughters also helped out – no sons lived
at Gad's Hill). Gossip circulated like wildfire fanned by Dickens's

Georgina Hogarth.

ill-advised public denunciation, in *The Times* no less, of certain 'abominable' rumours. Those in the know like Thackeray, who corrected his clubmates' misapprehensions, were aware that his mistress was 'an actress' (Georgina, those knowing ones also agreed, was the least handsome of the Hogarth girls).

Meanwhile the world at large assumed, very reasonably, that any misconduct must be with the woman Dickens had chosen to live with. Even after the wife's death, any such relationship, if sexual, was criminal. An illegitimate child (as many as three in wilder gossip) was speculated about. Grotesquely, Georgina felt obliged, in 1858, to procure a medical certificate of virginity. It is probable that Dickens coerced her into this painful business.

Whatever the facts of his domestic arrangements, Dickens would, since childhood, have been familiar with incest. As he passed through puberty he lived in houses in which (like that at Bayham Street, Camden – *see* 'Blue Plaques') large families were packed like rabbits in a hutch and were, inevitably, stimulated into rabbit-like promiscuities. There was no privacy, no separate sleeping arrangements. And, one presumes, illicit sex.

No reasonable person, looking at what evidence there is, will indict Dickens of this 'abomination'. He needs no certificate. But he knew abomination as a fact of Victorian life.

↬ Inimitable ↫

Dickens liked playfully to refer to himself as 'the Great Inimitable'. The title was first awarded him by his former schoolmaster, Mr Giles, in admiration for his pupil's *Pickwick Papers*. The nickname carried with it the implication that his work, like himself, was utterly 'original'. When he paid his fulsome tributes to Thomas Carlyle, it was because he was inspired by the other man, not derivative of him (*see* 'Carlylism').

On only one occasion in his life was Dickens plausibly accused of being culpably derivative – owing, that is, an unpaid debt to another artist.

After his death in 1870 – more specifically after John Forster's biography, which was grossly unfair to the illustrator George Cruikshank – the artist wrote a letter to *The Times* (30 December 1871) claiming that he 'originated' *Oliver Twist*. He did not mince his words. The novel, he asserted, 'was *entirely* my own idea and suggestion and all the characters are mine'.

An American admirer, four years earlier, had similarly claimed that the ideas for *Oliver Twist* had originated with the artist, not the writer. The charge infuriated Dickens and Forster, the

A Cruikshank illustration for *Oliver Twist*.

keeper of the Dickens flame. 'A monstrous absurdity', he called it. Dickensians, from Forster onwards, have universally nodded in agreement, often with the implication that Cruikshank was mad.

Dickens and Cruikshank had been brought together by Richard Bentley, for the grand launch of *Bentley's Miscellany*, in January 1837. Detailed knowledge of how the two men collaborated is frustrated by Forster's methodically destroying key pieces of evidence after he had used them. It's not his most admirable trait as a biographer. Loyalty to his subject is.

Is it the Dickensian equivalent of the 'Baconian heresy' on the authorship of Shakespeare? The distinguished Cruikshank scholar, Robert A. Vogler, makes a 'devil's advocate' case on behalf of his man. It depends on the following points:

1. Cruikshank worked via 'personal conferences' in which ideas were bounced to and fro ('brainstorming' in modern parlance). Other illustrators who worked for Dickens received instructions via peremptory letters. They worked 'for' not 'with' the Great Inimitable. Put another way, they did what they were damn well told. Cruikshank didn't work that way. After their first meeting Dickens reported that they had jointly hit on a 'capital idea'. Whose?

2. 'The idea that the best known illustrator in England at the age of 46, after having illustrated over 150 books, including the works of Smollett, Fielding, and Sterne, should submit drawings for approval to a 25-year-old author at the beginning of his career seems unlikely.'

3. The 'low life' subject matter, and themes, of *Oliver Twist* were a wholly new departure for the young author of *Pickwick*. Cruikshank had specialised in low-life scenes for decades.

4.   There exists a scrawled draft letter, from the period they were
     working together, in which Cruikshank asserts: 'the subject
     for the plates have been almost in every case etched before the
     author had written a line'.

As Vogler concludes, 'I have very seldom found Cruikshank
making statements that can be proven false'.

Cruikshank and Dickens never collaborated again after *Oliver
Twist*. Nor did Dickens ever again recruit an illustrator who could
plausibly claim to be his artistic equal.

↶ Insomnia ↷

Several Victorians contend for the title 'laureate of insomnia'.
Among them would be Dante Gabriel Rossetti, whose poem
'Insomnia' did much to popularise the term. James Thomson's
'City of Dreadful Night' envisions London as the kind of insom-
niac hell the earlier Dante might have rhapsodised about.

Dickens would also be a prime contender. Insomnia features
prominently in his narratives and is recorded as the state in which
he wrote some of his best work – the death of Jo in *Bleak House*, for
example, was created in a paroxysm of sleeplessness. The drugged
emergence into wakefulness in the opening of *Drood* is, plausibly, evidence of the desperate remedies the insomniac author was driven to.

Later in his life – in what is called (appropriately enough)
his 'dark period' – Dickens wrote the most sensitive analysis of
insomnia that the literature of his age can claim. It was 1861. His
marriage was in ruins. He had broken with his publisher. The
organic exhaustion that would eventually kill him was terminally
advanced. His sleep patterns had never been worse.

In his sleepless nights at this period, Dickens went on the tramp through London's night-time streets. The result was the collection of essays – nocturnes one might call them – published as *The Uncommercial Traveller*. They could as well be called, after St John, 'Dark Nights of the Soul'.

Most interesting is the piece 'Night Walks'. He would, Dickens records, rise from his sleepless bed and ramble round London till sunrise. The walk he describes from this particular night happens in March – an uncharitably raw and windy month. 'The wild moon and clouds were as restless as an evil conscience in a tumbled bed', he records.

As he leaves his own tumbled bed in Tavistock Square to walk the streets, looking at such things as river, the Houses of Parliament, the London slums, he realises he has never seen them as clearly as at this moment. It's as if a blind had been drawn. There is something else he feels on his night walk: Dickens calls it 'houselessness'.

'Expose thyself to feel what wretches feel', instructs King Lear. Dickens, as he walks the night streets, feels the companionship of the homeless, the wretched, the excluded masses of the world. In short, he feels his humanity, and the burden of it. We shall never know, but better sleep (a couple of Temazepams before turning in) might have robbed posterity of some great literature.

✌ Irishlessness ☞

A conundrum. Think of an Irishman or woman in Dickens's fiction. One could stretch a point and cite 'Micawber', whose name has a faint Hibernian tang to it, as does (some might say) its owner's fecklessness. But it's bricks without straw. (*See* 'Fagins'.)

It would be impossible to put together a book like this on Thackeray (think the O'Dowds in *Vanity Fair*), or Trollope (think Phineas Finn, 'the Irish member') without some reference to their interest in John Bull's Other Island. There was no JBOI for Dickens, apparently.

The Irish omission is particularly odd given what horrible things were going on across the Irish Sea in the 1840s. Thackeray, one notes, gave full exposure to the wretched peasantry in his *Irish Sketch Book* (1842). Trollope wrote articles for the London press during the great Irish famine, and introduced its horrors into his 1860 novel, *Castle Richmond*.

But for Dickens, as regards his fiction, there might as well have been no speck of land between Liverpool and New York harbours. The Irish and Ireland are invisible. On one occasion, however, the cockney scales did drop from his eyes. This was on his first visit to America.

He could not ignore the Irish there, because they were in the process of building the place. Nor had the melting pot yet dissolved their national characteristics (Israel Zangwill, one of Dickens's most distinguished disciples, came up with the 'melting pot' image for America's great social blending). Dickens describes two labourers in *American Notes*, the book he wrote on his return to England:

Irishmen both! You might know them, if they were masked, by their long-tailed blue coats and bright buttons, and their drab trousers, which they wear like men well used to working dresses, who are easy in no others. It would be hard to keep your model republics going, without the countrymen and countrywomen of those two labourers. For who else would dig, and delve, and drudge, and do domestic work, and make canals and roads, and execute great lines of Internal Improvement!

He could see this, and hail it, in America: but oddly not in his own country, where an army of Irish navvies were building the railways and roads on which he travelled, and millions perishing of hunger in their homeland. *Dombey and Son* records, at great length, the laying of train lines into London. Scarcely a shovel that did that heroic work wasn't wielded by an Irishman. Yet there is only one reference to 'Irish' in the novel – and that is to imported Irish linen. It's odd.

৵ Itch Ward ৵

Some terms one is glad to have dropped out of the language because there is no longer any use for them. What they once referred to no longer exists. Thank God.

'Itch Ward' is one such term.

Not one reader of Dickens in a thousand, I suspect, will understand it without helpful annotation. It was where inmates with venereal disease, or their luckless tainted offspring, were quarantined in workhouses, to rot. The name itself indicates the lack of sympathy for such unfortunates.

A letter of 12 May 1850 from Dickens records a visit he made with a friend, Jacob Bell, to a workhouse for an essay for his paper, *Household Words*. As he told Bell, 'I have thought a great deal about that woman, the Wardswoman [i.e. nurse] in the Itch Ward'. The workhouse in question was the Clapham and Wandsworth institution. It contained 2,000 paupers. As Dickens recorded in 'A Walk in the Workhouse', they ranged from 'the infant newly born or not yet to come into the pauper world, to the old man dying in his bed'.

It was all unutterably depressing – none of it more so than the Itch Ward, which presented a scene 'worthy of Hogarth'. Dickens gives a vivid pen-portrait of the wardswoman he and Bell had encountered there. She was 'herself a pauper – flabby, raw-boned, untidy – unpromising and coarse of aspect as need be'. No surprise there. But, oddly, the woman was 'crying inconsolably'.

What was the matter with the nurse of the itch-ward? Oh, 'the dropped child' was dead! Oh, the child that was found in the street, and she had brought up ever since, had died an hour ago, and see where the little creature lay, beneath this cloth! The dear, the pretty dear!

The dropped child seemed too small and poor a thing for Death to be in earnest with, but Death had taken it; and already its diminutive form was neatly washed, composed, and stretched as if in sleep upon a box.

One cannot but be glad for the modern reader's ignorance. 'Itch Ward? What on earth's that? Never heard of such a thing.' Good riddance, one responds.

⤷ Keynotes ⤶

'Strike the Keynote!' Dickens would instruct himself in his 'memoranda' for whatever novel he was writing. We would probably use the terms 'leitmotif', or 'dominating symbol'. But it's clear that he meant the heart of the enterprise.

Dickens's working notes are fascinating windows into genius at work. He did not blueprint his future novel, like an architect or engineer. He jotted down 'memoranda' that kept the future evolution of the plot open, flexible, and organic. Because his notes, scrupulous as they are, avoid long-term forecast, we have not the slightest idea how the novel *Edwin Drood*, cut off halfway through by his death, was to end.

Nonetheless Dickens was very careful (after his early days as a novelist, when he did rather wing it) to identify the 'keynote' before he began to write. This is evident in the great care he gave his titles. Take the following notes he made for himself on the trial title for what was to be *Hard Times* (but could have been called many other things) before composition:

Stubborn Things

Fact

Thomas Gradgrind's facts

~~George~~ John Gradgrind's facts

Hard-headed Gradgrind

The Grindstone

Hard heads and soft hearts

The Time Grinders

~~Mr Gradgrind's grindstone~~

~~Hard Times~~

The ~~universal~~ grindstone

Hard Times

Heads and Tales

Two and two are four

Prove it!

Black and white

/According to Cocker [author of an arithmetic school book]

/Prove it!

Stubborn things

/~~Facts are stubborn things~~

Mr Gradgrind's ~~grindstone~~ facts
/The ~~John Thomas Thomas Mr Gradgrind's~~ grindstone
Hard Times
/Two and two are four
/~~Calculations~~
~~According to Cocker~~
~~Damaging Facts~~
/Something tangible
/Our hard-headed friend
/Rust and dust

Dickens sent a sample of these trial titles to John Forster and another friend. They plumped for *Hard Times*. If he'd asked me I would have gone for 'Rust and Dust'. More Dickensian, to my ear.

∾ Killer ∽

Dickens never restrained his homicidal instincts in his fiction. 'Kill Gaffer *retributively*' he instructed himself in his notes for *Our Mutual Friend*. The old corpse-fisher should himself sleep with the fishes – not that the filthy waters of the Thames would support any marine life for another 150 years. A mouthful was more lethal than arsenic.

There is a similarly chilling memorandum in Dickens's private notes for *Bleak House*:

Mr Tulkinghorn to be shot (Pointing Roman)
George to be taken by Bucket. Yes.
Jo? Yes. Kill him.

One can almost hear Dickens's mind popping and fizzing at such moments. For just a moment, that little boy's life was in Dickens's hand. He could have had Jo cured of his fatal fever and had it revealed – in the last chapter of the novel – that he was an illegitimate son of Sir Leicester Dedlock.

But no. Dickens decided to 'kill him'.

Did Dickens kill anyone outside his fiction (other than himself, by hard work)? Arguably his whole wonderful career depended on his killing a man who stood in his way.

The process by which Dickens was launched into overnight fame is legendary. He was recruited by Chapman & Hall to supply letter press (supporting text) for a series of cockney 'sporting plates', chronicling the comic accidents with gun, rod and horse of a 'Nimrod Club' (Nimrod being the great hunter in the Bible).

The series was to be centred on the venerable illustrator, Robert Seymour. Dickens was hired at the low pay rate of £14 per month. He was not the first choice. As sportsmen say, when two men ride a horse, one must ride behind. That was where young Dickens (fifteen years Seymour's junior) was expected to be. Behind.

But not for long. There ensued a series of quarrels. Dickens won every point. As the third number was in press, the two men had their only meeting, at which, over a glass of grog, Dickens gave instructions that the sporting theme should be dropped and (it has been alleged) suggested that Seymour might be dropped as well. Three days later Seymour took his fowling piece (a sportsman's gun), went to his studio at the bottom of his garden, and shot himself in the heart. The rest is literary history.

Seymour was still in his thirties. He left a note to his wife: 'Best and dearest of wives – for such you have been to me – blame, I charge you, no one.' She did in fact blame someone: Charles

Seymour illustrates *Pickwick* – briefly.

Dickens; or 'Boz' as the young puppy called himself, who had erected his wonderful career on her husband's grave.

In July 2010 it was reported that Seymour's neglected tombstone had been acquired to go on permanent display at the Dickens Museum, 48 Doughty Street, London. As *The Guardian* reported:

> At the museum, which is planning celebrations for the bicentenary of Dickens' birth in 1812, the director, Florian Schweizer, said: 'We welcome the monument as an important addition to our collections – but I don't think one can blame Dickens for his death at all.'

Some do.

❧ King Charles's Head ☙

Some chips of the great Dickensian block have flown off from their novels to take on an independent life. If, until a few years ago, you had asked someone who had never read *Martin Chuzzlewit* what a 'gamp' was, they would have told you: 'an umbrella'. (*See* 'Gamp'.) So too with 'King Charles's Head', a byword for 'personal obsession'.

It originates in *David Copperfield*, at that point in the early narrative when the hero, like Mr Dick, has taken refuge in Betsey Trotwood's cottage (Dickens associated cottages with safety and benevolence, hence 'Urania Cottage' – *see* 'Home for the Homeless'). For ten years, David discovers, Mr Dick has been wrestling with a petition he intends to submit to the Lord Chancellor (a public figure soon to be skewered in *Bleak House*, for whom ten years in setting things straight is the mere blink of an eye). Mr Dick's plea concerns some public memorial, or statue, that should be raised. But he can never finish what he is writing because King Charles's Head keeps taking over his own head. As David discovers:

> Every day of his life he had a long sitting at the Memorial, which never made the least progress, however hard he laboured, for King Charles the First always strayed into it, sooner or later, and then it was thrown aside, and another one begun.

Mr Dick is a monomaniac – a theory in that pre-Freudian time popularised by the French psychiatrist Esquirol.

Betsey explains it in layman's terms to David:

> 'Ah!' said my aunt, rubbing her nose as if she were a little vexed. 'That's his allegorical way of expressing it. He connects his

illness with great disturbance and agitation, naturally, and that's the figure, or the simile, or whatever it's called, which he chooses to use.'

It's what Freud calls 'displacement activity'.

The manuscript shows that Dickens originally had a 'bull in a china shop' as Mr Dick's *idée fixe*. Why did he change it? The superficial explanation is that he was writing in 1849 and that year was the 200th anniversary of the king's execution. Bicentenaries (as 2012 witnesses with Dickens himself) put famous names back into circulation.

There was a second reason in that 1848 (the 'year of revolutions' across Europe) had seen a 'second French Revolution'. Chopping off royal heads was back on national agendas.

There was a third, sly, reason buried rather deeper in the narrative fabric. *Charles* Head/Mr *Dick* throws back an obvious echo. Crossword puzzle-solvers will have no difficulty, either, in connecting the reverse initials D[avid] C[opperfield] and C[harles] D[ickens]. Mirrors throw back reversed images. And *David Copperfield* is Dickens's most autobiographical novel.

✌ Madame Guillotine ❧

The words for the traditional instruments of execution in France are feminine: *la corde* (the rope) and *la hache* (the axe). The most characteristically French instrument of execution is, of course, *la guillotine*.

The apparatus was introduced to the Revolutionary authorities by Dr Joseph-Ignace Guillotin as something that circumvented the old class privilege of the axe for nobles and the rope for commoners. It was rational and – insofar as cutting someone's head off can be – humane; unlike, for example, the exotically barbarous *ancien régime* treatment of Robert-François Damiens (*see* 'Punishment'). Or even the lynching from lamp-posts ('à la lanterne!') that had marred initial outbreaks of Revolutionary violence.

Breaking on the wheel, burning at the stake, and quartering (still practised in England, as Jerry Cruncher complains in *A Tale of Two Cities*, denying him corpses to sell) belonged to the pre-Revolutionary past. The guillotine was also devilishly efficient – permitting the mass extermination of a whole class. The last was particularly attractive and in 1792 the Assembly passed a decree making the guillotine the only legal form of execution.

But why, given its origin, was it not called *le guillotin*? Why is *guillotine* feminised, much more so than the rope and axe, where the gender is merely formal? No convincing linguistic answer has been offered (in Germany, incidentally, where it was enthusiastically adopted by Hitler, *das Fallbeil* is neuter).

Dickens was fascinated by the chopping-machine's gender. It's not merely linguistically feminine but sexually so. The point is stressed throughout *A Tale of Two Cities*, in such passing comments as:

> The word 'wife' seemed to serve as a gloomy reminder to Defarge, to say with sudden impatience, 'In the name of that sharp female newly-born, and called La Guillotine, why did you come to France?'

The phrase 'sharp female' recurs frequently, as does 'Madame Guillotine'. It is one of the novel's keynotes (*see* 'Keynotes'). The

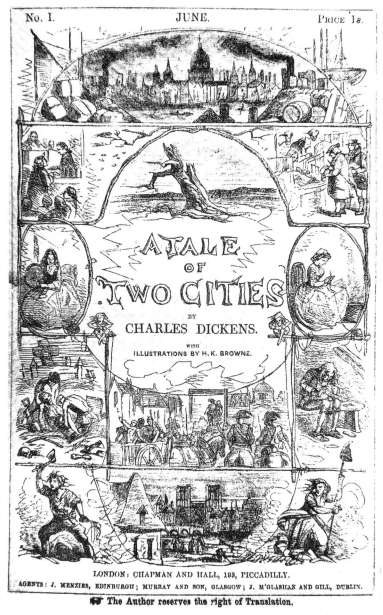

Serial wrapper illustration for *A Tale of Two Cities*.

tone of the references is odd. At one point Dickens launches into a virtuosic cascade of sick guillotine jokes of the kind that would never have been permissible about Jack Ketch's good old English noose:

> It was the popular theme for jests; it was the best cure for headache, it infallibly prevented the hair from turning grey, it imparted a peculiar delicacy to the complexion, it was the National Razor which shaved close: who kissed La Guillotine, looked through the little window and sneezed into the sack.

The fascination, emotional excitement and the femininity suggest, inescapably, that subliminally the guillotine implied to the male mind not decapitation but castration. More so with those women ('tricoteuses') sitting by the machine, imperturbably *knitting* (for God's sake!), 'never faltering or pausing in their Work' as men's vital parts are chopped off and fall into the basket.

৩৩ Marshalsea ৩৩

There are prison walls everywhere in Dickens. Three actual jails predominate: Newgate, the Bastille, and the Marshalsea debtors' prison in Southwark.

The last was the prison he knew best – his family having been incarcerated there for a few months in 1824. Like Philoctetes' heel, that wound never healed, but stank and suppurated through his life. It forms the dynamic centre of what is now regarded as one of the finest novels of his 'dark period', *Little Dorrit*. 'It is gone now', he writes in Chapter 6 (the prison was closed by Act of Parliament in 1842). But for him the Marshalsea never went.

From memory, where it was as real to his eye as the paper he was writing on, he describes the place:

> It was an oblong pile of barrack building, partitioned into squalid houses standing back to back, so that there were no back rooms; environed by a narrow paved yard, hemmed in by high walls duly spiked at top. Itself a close and confined prison for debtors, it contained within it a much closer and more confined jail for smugglers. Offenders against the revenue laws, and defaulters to excise or customs who had incurred fines which they were unable to pay, were supposed to be incarcerated behind an iron-plated door closing up a second prison.

Also confined there were those guilty of 'unnatural crimes'. 'Children?' says the turnkey to William Dorrit as he is taken in, 'and the rules? Why, lord set you up like a corner pin, we've a reg'lar playground of them. Children? Why, we swarm with 'em.' The play goes beyond ring a ring of roses, one suspects. Given the free and easy regime, sex was not controlled. Prostitution and rape were rife. And, doubtless, paedophilia.

As the novel goes on to describe, it was a very strange kind of prison. Its *raison d'être* was not punitive like Newgate, or curative like Pentonville (*see* 'Punishment'), but merely confinement. You were, as old lags put it, 'inside'; 'banged up'. Not just you, but whole families (the unindebted were given free egress and regress). Apartments were available for 'collegians' who could stump up the 'garnish'. Since debtors, a main constituent in the Marshalsea population, could earn nothing, they might serve inordinately long sentences – life, even – for trivial offences (a baker's bill, in John Dickens's case).

For William Dorrit, the 'amiable and helpless middle-aged gentleman' who has, by virtue of long incarceration, become 'the father of the Marshalsea', the prison is his world. For his daughter, 'the child of the Marshalsea', imprisonment – like the emery used to polish precious stones – has brought out the inherent goodness of her character. Aged 22, as the novel begins, she is released into the 'Free City'. But will she ever be free? Was her creator, Dickens, a son of the Marshalsea, ever set free?

৩ Megalosaurus ৫৩

Bleak House opens with a bleak panorama of Holborn with the inevitable (whether 1852 or 2012) traffic jam.

> London. Michaelmas term lately over, and the Lord Chancellor sitting in Lincoln's Inn Hall. Implacable November weather. As much mud in the streets as if the waters had but newly retired from the face of the earth, and it would not be wonderful to meet a megalosaurus, forty feet long or so, waddling like an elephantine lizard up Holborn Hill.

It would, in point of fact, be rather wonderful. The novelist is here playing with traditional creation myths (primal soup, primal chaos, etc.). It is not in all points the version of creation handed down by Genesis. One can, fancifully, see a premonition of Darwin. Dickens was an early reader when the *Origin of Species* came out, seven years later (*see* 'Darwin').

In the context of March 1852, however, when the first instalment of *Bleak House* hit Mr W.H. Smith's stands ('First with the News: First with Dickens'), readers would have recalled the Great

Exhibition, just a few months earlier. Among the wonderful sights that all the world came to see at Hyde Park and the 'Crystal Palace' in summer 1851 were the *papier-mâché* dinosaurs modelled by Robert Owen, the father of modern palaeontology. It was Owen who came up with the name 'Dinosauria', or 'terrible lizards', and reconstructed what they looked like from bones being dug up.

Owen's designs (at the behest of Prince Albert, no less) were sculpted in concrete by Benjamin Hawkins for the Great Exhibition (Albert's brainchild). They were installed, along with the Crystal Palace itself, in Sydenham Park, south of London, in 1854. So while *Bleak House* was in serial publication, a megalo-saurus really was wandering across the capital.

The Owen–Hawkins monsters – located in the undergrowth on an island in the park lake – have delighted children for 150 years. These terrible lizards must, however, have disturbed Victorian parents. It's easier to find a home for them in Sydenham Park than in Genesis.

How on earth (literally) did those dinosaurs disappear? Desperate Christian fundamentalists in America have argued that they were too big for Noah's ark – hence extinction by flood. But not all dinosaurs were large (one thinks of those nasty little velociraptors in Spielberg's *Jurassic Park*).

It was troubling. That unease, one suspects, was a fore-tremor of the earthquake to come, on 24 November 1859, when Mr Darwin's book was released to the world.

∽ Merrikins ∾

Dickens detested three things American: (1) the American spit-toon, (2) the American toothpick, and (3) the American love of picking his pocket while expecting Boz to be profoundly grateful for the privilege of being relieved of his hard-won literary earnings. Nor did he have much time for slavery and Yankee cock-a-doodle-dandy pride in not being British.

Himself a journalist, Dickens was also profoundly unimpressed by the American press and such jewels in its crown as (his names) the *New York Sewer*, the *New York Stabber*, and the *New York Keyhole Peeper*. When American newspapers were sent to him he had them burned unread.

There was a long line of English writers profitably 'blowin' up the Merrikins' (as Sam Weller puts it in *The Pickwick Papers*) going back to Mrs Trollope's sublimely rude 1834 bestseller *The Domestic Manners of the Americans* (they have none – she too was appalled by the overflowing spittoon and publicly wielded toothpick). Dickens, after a relatively polite anatomy of the Great Republic in *American Notes* (the record of his 1842 visit) gave full vent to Yankee mannerlessness in *Martin Chuzzlewit* (serialised January 1843–July 1844).

Martin crosses the Atlantic on the 'Screw'. It is an aptly named vessel. In God's Own Country the young man is screwed out of his cash by villainous American realtors and poisoned by that pestilential stream, the Mississippi.

The country also (as he angrily believed) screwed Dickens. A much-repeated vignette testifying to American Bozmania is that of the stevedores on the New York docks shouting to the incoming steamer (among whose cargo were 'early sheets' of Dickens's latest serial): 'Is she dead yet?' Little Nell, that is. None of those husky fans would have remitted a plug nickel to Dickens's bank account (Coutts) via their pirated copies of *The Old Curiosity Shop*. America did not sign up to International Copyright until a quarter of a century after Dickens's death.

Little Nell at rest.

Dickens made a second trip to the United States from November 1867 to April 1868, when his sensationally popular public readings yielded £19,000. It was dangerously earned money. His pulse rate during the readings soared to explosive levels. On his return he suffered a mild stroke, the harbinger of the aneurysm that killed him two years later. America had its revenge for *Chuzzlewit*.

✺ Micawberomics ✺

Mr Micawber's sage advice to David Copperfield about money is much quoted.

'Annual income twenty pounds, annual expenditure nineteen nineteen and six, result happiness. Annual income twenty pounds, annual expenditure twenty pounds ought and six, result misery. The blossom is blighted, the leaf is withered, the god of day goes down upon the dreary scene, and – and in short you are for ever floored. As I am!'

To make his example the more impressive, Mr Micawber drank a glass of punch with an air of great enjoyment and satisfaction, and whistled the College Hornpipe.

He promptly cadges a shilling (two sixpences) from David.

Dickens confided the origin of this comic scene, uncomically, to his biographer John Forster. He had, still a boy, visited his father in Marshalsea debtors' prison:

[He] was waiting for me in the lodge, and we went up to his room (on the top storey but one), and cried very much. And he told me, I remember, to take warning by the Marshalsea, and to observe that if a man had twenty pounds a year and spent nineteen pounds nineteen shillings and sixpence, he would be happy; but that a shilling spent the other way would make him wretched. I see the fire we sat before, now; with two bricks inside the rusted grate, one on each side, to prevent its burning too many coals.

Mr Micawber's system points to a contradiction in Dickens's thinking about money. If Scrooge, as regenerated by the Christmas ghosts, persists in throwing his money away he will find himself in the Marshalsea alongside John Dickens. There was no future in the London money-lending trade, then as now, for warm-hearted loan sharks.

In his personal life Dickens was prudent, if not quite miserly. Having been rejected as too poor (financially) a suitor for the banker's daughter Maria Beadnell, he married his editor's daughter. He allowed Angela Burdett-Coutts – the second-richest woman in England – to take over payment for the career (Eton, Barings Bank) of his eldest son and heir, Charles. When he removed Mrs Dickens from his life he did so on a stipend of £600 a year. He was, at the same time, signing book contracts for £10,000 (over £1,000,000 in today's money) and was, probably, the richest man of letters in Britain.

On his death, Dickens left £93,000. Or, put another way, 3,720,000 Micawberish sixpences.

Mr Micawber.

৵৯ **Mist** ৫৹

Which is the mistiest of Dickens's novels? No contest: *Great Expectations*. The white stuff wreathes the narrative and swirls around all its main events. The opening scene strikes the keynote, as Dickens liked to say. The seven-year-old Pip is found regarding the seven gravestones of his siblings and parents (was ever child more lonely?) on Christmas Eve (was ever Christmas, even Scrooge's, more wretched?).

Mist is creeping in from the marshes. What awaits the little fellow in his life to come? By way of answer a murderer leaps out from behind the grave of his father.

Move to the end of the novel (as printed). It finds Pip and Estella in the ruined garden of ruined Satis House. They have met there by chance – will their ways part again? The novel does not tell us, shrouding the future in unpredictability:

> I took her hand in mine, and we went out of the ruined place; and, as the morning mists had risen long ago when I first left the forge, so, the evening mists were rising now, and in all the broad expanse of tranquil light they showed to me, I saw no shadow of another parting from her.

But, one wonders, what can you 'see' in mist? Just mist.

Mist, one must stress, is a different commodity from fog in Dickensian meteorology. It is not urban, but rural – it rises, most typically, from marsh and river at dawn and dusk. Mist is not, like Dickensian fog, poisonous. It symbolises the inherent mystery ('mistery', one is tempted to pun) of our existence.

Mist is found everywhere in Dickens and it typically inspires some of his finest verbal painting. The following is a striking example, from *Our Mutual Friend* (Chapter 57):

> Day was breaking at Plashwater Weir Mill Lock. Stars were yet
> visible, but there was dull light in the east that was not the light
> of night. The moon had gone down, and a mist crept along the
> banks of the river, seen through which the trees were the ghosts
> of trees, and the water was the ghost of water. This earth looked
> spectral, and so did the pale stars: while the cold eastern glare,
> expressionless as to heat or colour, with the eye of the firmament
> quenched, might have been likened to the stare of the dead.

Substitute 'fog' for 'mist' in such passages and the power
evaporates.

One of the most gripping scenes in *Great Expectations* is that
when Pip has been lured by Old Orlick to the deserted lime-kiln
on the misty marshes (yet again). Orlick intends to strangle Pip
and incinerate his corpse. A white vapour, swirling over the places
he once lived, Pip grimly foresees, is all that will remain of him. He
will have less substance even than Marley's ghost. Perhaps Estella
will breathe him.

Pip, fortuitously, is rescued. His misty destiny (with Estella?
Without her?) is postponed, but still in that last scene, about which
Dickens was so uncertain – he wrote three versions – unseeable.

৩ **Murder** ৎ

Murder is everywhere in Dickens. So much so that one can pro-
pose a *Cluedo* puzzle around it. One should, however, mark this
entry with 'Spoiler Alert!!' for readers who have not yet read the
whodunits.

1. Who is murdered in the office with a rifle?

2. Who is murdered in the garret with a billyclub?

3. Who is murdered in the Thames with bare hands?

4. Who is murdered by a horse?

5. Who is murdered in a cathedral with an unknown instrument?

6. Who is murdered at the lock with a bear hug?

7. Who do we think poisoned his father in his bedroom, and who did he really murder, and who does he really poison, and where?

8. Who murders his wife by throwing her over a cliff?

9. What would-be murderer has his poisoned brandy thrown back in his face by his planned victim, in legal chambers?

10. Who was murdered, 22 years ago, in his bed, with a severed alarm cord in his hand?

Answers: 1. The sinister lawyer, Tulkinghorn, in *Bleak House*. Rouncewell is instantly suspected. Hortense, the French maid, is the actual guilty party. 2. Poor Nancy from *Oliver Twist*. Her heart is pure and her battered head has Rose's pure white hanky (unused) as its shroud. 3. Magwitch finally gets to strangle his lifelong foe, Compeyson, in the Thames in *Great Expectations*. 4. Bentley Drummle, also in *Great Expectations*. Good thing too. 5. No one is too sure about this, as the novel remained unfinished – but Dickens supposedly told his biographer John Forster that Jasper was going to murder Edwin Drood this way. 6. In *Our Mutual Friend*, Bradley Headstone grips Rogue Riderhood (the man who cannot drown – having 'drowned' once) in a ring of iron, and takes him down into the depths of the river. Good riddance to both of them. 7. Jonas Chuzzlewit believes he has murdered his father this way (he hasn't), he later actually kills Tigg, and finally poisons himself on the way to jail. 8. Rigaud Blandois confesses to this crime in the jail scene at the opening of *Little Dorrit*. 9. Julius Slinkton, owner of the most unpleasant name in Dickens's fiction, in *Hunted Down*. 10. Reuben Haredale in *Barnaby Rudge*.

∽ Nomenclature ∾

Henry James observed that of all the great Victorian novelists, Thackeray was the most 'perfect' in the creation of names for his characters. For example: Sir Pitt Crawley (combination of ambitious politician and toady), the Marquess of Steyne (Regency Brighton, 'stain'), etc. Trollope, James thought, was abysmal in this respect. Dickens? Good and bad.

Thackeray was wholly scornful of his rival's skills in this department. As he told a friend: 'I quarrel with Dickens's art in many respects; which I don't think represents Nature truly; for instance Micawber seems to me an exaggeration of a man, as his name is of a name.' It is true that at times Dickens does come up with ineffably lame names, although Micawber is by no means the lamest. In the shame-name list one would place highest: M'Choakumchild for a teacher who crams his pupils and Wackford Squeers for a teacher who aims at their buttocks rather than their brains. Cratchit, for a scrivener who spends his life scratching with a pen; Bounderby for a self-made man who is jumped-up; Biddy for a woman who is eminently biddable; or Veneering for a couple who are socially shallow, are all passable, but by no means in the Thackeray class.

There is one area, however, in which Dickens is expert – namely names that embody deniable scatological or obscene hints. In *Oliver Twist* Charley Bates is the only one of Fagin's crew given the title 'Master' – thus evoking the joke that was current in my school playground, and must, evidently, have been in Dickens's: 'This is Mr and Mrs Bates, and their son Master Bates.' Murdstone and Merdle (*see* 'Street-Sweepings') evoke the French *merde*. They are truly shitty characters. Merdle deals, of course, in 'filthy lucre'.

'Uriah Heep' brings with it, every time the name and its owner crop up in *David Copperfield*, a subliminal vision of a heap of ordure ('uria' is defined in the dictionary as 'urine'; and 'urea', even less attractively, as 'the solid component of mammalian urine'). Likewise 'Carker' and 'cack' (a slang term for excrement). One does not have to read much Victorian pornography to make a connection between Rosa Bud and nipples.

Of course the kind of reader Dickens most admires would never catch these unworthy echoes. I, alas, do.

Uriah, as unlovely as his name.

৩ Ohm's Law ৫

Dickens made a tellingly Dickensian remark to his wife after reading one of his Christmas stories, 'The Chimes', to a group of friends in 1844:

[I]f you had seen [Daniel] Maclise last night – undisguisedly sobbing, and crying on the sofa as I read – you would have felt (as I did) what a thing it is to have *Power*.

It's an odd word in this context. Writers usually hope to have 'influence' not 'power'. In using it Dickens was probably thinking about electricity (which fascinated him) rather than sexual potency or political power. In his management of his journals he habitually used the similarly electrical-sounding word 'conductor' rather than 'editor'.

Electricity, as any school child knows, weakens in proportion to the distance it is conducted between two points. This is Ohm's Law.

Dickens's professional career can be seen as an attempt to shorten that length, and the resistance it incurred. He broke with his first publishers, Chapman & Hall, and his second, Richard Bentley, and in the early 1840s transferred his business to Bradbury & Evans with the explanation that 'a printer is better than a bookseller'. Why better? Because it represented one 'middle-man' less. Less 'resistance' to the powerful Dickensian current.

But even this short cut brought with it too much resistance. Dickens himself set up as a publisher (of his and others' work) in his papers *Household Words* and *All the Year Round*. 'There is no publisher whatever associated with *All the Year Round*', he declared.

Dickens reading 'The Chimes'.

But as he entered his last decade, the printed page, even those publisherless ones he printed himself, created more resistance than he could live with. He closed the circuits completely with the celebrated public readings to which he devoted the last years of his life – it was, of course, the same situation as all those years ago with 'The Chimes', when he had first discovered his 'Power'.

❧ Onions ☙

If there was an *annus horribilis* in Dickens's life 1860 would be a strong candidate. His marriage had broken down irreparably and adulterously. The bad publicity besmirched his public image – not helped by his own injudicious addresses to his loyal public through the national press about 'some domestic trouble of mine'.

He was about to embark on an illicit relationship which, if it got out, would destroy him. Details were swirling around those in the know in London: 'not his sister-in-law, an actress', Thackeray blubbed to his club friends, unable to keep the confidential information in his mouth.

Dickens had broken with his publisher, with many of his friends, and with the majority of his ten children on the grounds of his gross mistreatment of their mother, Catherine. He was moving to a new house, Gad's Hill, the only residence he would ever own, while keeping up a base in London and an expensive love nest for his mistress Nelly (Ellen Ternan) outside London. He was uncertain that even with his massive income he could keep himself afloat financially. He embarked on a health-ruining series of public readings to keep himself safely solvent.

It was, in short, a bad time. He would, he resolved, make sure that no snooper could dig into those records that he was still able to destroy. On 4 September 1860 he told his sub-editor on *Household Words*, W.H. Wills: 'Yesterday I burnt, in the field at Gad's Hill, the accumulated letters and papers of twenty years.' The scene is painted vividly in all the standard biographies, drawing on the eye-witness testimony, recollected much later, by his daughter Katey. She, now a teenager, and her young brothers Henry (aged eleven) and 'Plorn' (aged eight) lugged out basket after basket of biographer's gold. Katey asked her father to spare a few scraps. He replied along the lines: 'Would to God every letter I had ever written was on that pile.'

His justification for the conflagration was given to his actor friend, William Macready, a year later:

Daily seeing improper uses made of confidential letters, in the addressing of them to a public audience that has no business with them, I made, not long ago, a great fire in my field at Gad's Hill, and burnt every letter I possessed. And now I always destroy every letter I receive – not on absolute business, and my mind is, so far, at ease.

So massive was the fire that his children, as Henry later recalled, 'roasted onions on the ashes of the great!' All that was left for those 90-plus biographers and their successors was cold ashes. No onions for them.

(PS. Recent research has proved, beyond doubt, that Katey was not at this bonfire and it's extremely unlikely the other children were. And it was pelting with rain on the day Dickens claimed to have had his fire. Every Dickensian biographer is, alas, on thin ice.)

∽ Peckham Conjectures ∾

Dickens specialised in death scenes. We have, thanks to his sister-in-law Georgina, his housekeeper, a graphic recollection of his own. Graphic but, some claim, dubious.

In early summer 1870 Charles Dickens was, manifestly, a sick man. He had suffered minor strokes. His body was breaking down. Nonetheless on the morning of the 8th of June he was observed by Georgina to be 'in excellent spirits'. He spent the sunny morning in his writing chalet at the foot of the Gad's Hill garden, penning the description of Rochester in glorious summer from *Edwin Drood*, which begins: 'Brilliant morning shines on the old city …'

That night he wrote some letters before dinner. During the meal – at which only Georgina shared the table – he was visibly ill. It was the onset of a catastrophic stroke:

He continued to talk, but incoherently and very indistinctly. It being now evident that he was in a serious condition, [Georgina] begged him to go to his room before she sent for medical aid. 'Come and lie down,' she entreated. 'Yes, on the ground,' he answered indistinctly. These were the last words that he uttered.

His personal physician and close confidant, Frank Beard, was sent for. Dickens survived the night, insensibly. Late on the 9th, two specialists were called from London. It was hopeless. He died at ten minutes past six that day. The necessary announcements were made and the nation was plunged into grief.

Not old, but looking old.

Biographers, from John Forster onwards (who had his account directly from Georgina), have faithfully followed this story. But was it true? There had long been rumours that Georgina's version was a cover-up. Claire Tomalin examines them carefully and judiciously in the paperback edition of her biography of Ellen Ternan, Dickens's mistress, and in her 2011 biography of Dickens. The rumours now have the status of an alternative if still controversial truth.

The Peckham conjecture, as it's called, runs thus. Dickens was actually in the house (possibly the bed) of Ellen Ternan – this being the house he had acquired for her in south London – when he suffered his stroke. She telegrammed Georgina with the necessary precautionary codes, and the patient was transported by carriage to Gad's Hill. Frank Beard – one of the Dickens inner circle – Georgina and Ellen concocted the official version in the almost 24 hours they had available. The servants' lips (those that may have picked up something) were sealed.

A number of Dickensians (notably Michael Slater in his 2009 biography) pooh-pooh the Peckham conjecture. The fact is that we shall never know. But, post-Tomalin, we shall always wonder.

♥ Perambulation ♥

Dickens was a phenomenal walker. He thought nothing of walking the 30 miles from his London house to his country house in Rochester at his brisk four miles an hour. Walks feature centrally in his fiction. One recalls Oliver Twist walking (from Rochester, alias Mudfog) to London; Little Nell and her grandfather, ever walking until the poor girl can walk no more; Lady Dedlock in *Bleak House*, making her last doomed walk all the way from the West End to St Albans and back, to get one last look at her daughter (which, sadly, she doesn't); Pip walking the two miles to Satis House, or the five miles to the graveyard where his family lie, in *Great Expectations*. Shanks's pony is locomotion found in every novel.

Dickens's earliest book, *Sketches by Boz*, is the record of walks around London. In a later perambulatory work, *The Uncommercial Traveller*, he notes wryly of himself:

> So much of my travelling is done on foot, that if I cherished betting propensities, I should probably be found registered in sporting newspapers under some such title as the Elastic Novice, challenging all eleven stone mankind to competition in walking.

He goes on to tell us:

> My walking is of two kinds: one, straight on end to a definite goal at a round pace; one, objectless, loitering, and purely vaga-bond. In the latter state, no gipsy on earth is a greater vagabond than myself; it is so natural to me, and strong with me, that I think I must be the descendant, at no great distance, of some irreclaimable tramp.

An American friend leaves us a record of what it was like taking a walk with Boz:

> His favourite mode of exercise was walking; and when in America … scarcely a day passed, no matter what the weather, that he did not accomplish his eight or ten miles. It was on these expeditions that he liked to recount to the companion of his rambles stories and incidents of his early life; and when he was in the mood, his fun and humour knew no bounds. He would then frequently discuss the

numerous characters in his delightful books, and would act out, on the road, dramatic situations, where Nickleby or Copperfield or Swiveller would play distinguished parts.

On his last day of conscious life, it is pleasant to record, Dickens allowed himself one relaxation from his work. He went for a long walk in the June sunshine.

ᥩ Pies ᥩ

Simple Simon met a pieman,
Going to the fair;
Says Simple Simon to the pieman,
Let me taste your ware.

It's a nursery rhyme going back, at least, to the eighteenth century. It was quite likely one of the first things the infant Charles Dickens warbled.

In his time (even ours, if one thinks about it) only simpletons were not careful about the pieman's wares. That carrion – even human flesh – might be in that tasty meat dish is a legendary horror going all the way back to Thyestes in Greek myth. Dickens was, like all his contemporaries, instinctively tuned in to the urban legend. The aroma of the appetising pie, of dubious content, is frequently encountered in his fiction.

Tony Weller, for example, tells Mr Pickwick (always careful to 'investigate the interior' of any pie he is eating, one notes):

'I lodged in the same house vith a pieman once, sir, and a wery nice man he was – reg'lar clever chap, too – make pies out

o' anything, he could. "What a number o' cats you keep, Mr
Brooks," says I, when I'd got intimate with him. "Ah," says he, "I
do – a good many," says he. "You must be wery fond o' cats," says
I. "Other people is," says he, a-winkin' at me … "Mr Weller," says
he, a-squeezing my hand wery hard, and vispering in my ear –
"don't mention this here agin – but it's the seasonin' as does it.
They're all made o' them noble animals," says he, a-pointin' to
a wery nice little tabby kitten, "and I seasons 'em for beefsteak,
weal or kidney, 'cording to the demand.'"

PHIZ. fecit

Tony Weller.

The Dancers (brother and sister) make their pies out of dead sheep they find when out walking ('roadkill') in *Our Mutual Friend*. In *Martin Chuzzlewit*, Tom Pinch is described musing on the same topic of the questionable pie, after he too has been out walking too long:

> 'Upon my word,' thought Tom, quickening his pace, 'I don't know what John will think has become of me. He'll begin to be afraid I have strayed into one of those streets where the country-men are murdered; and that I have been made meat pies of, or some such horrible thing.'

In *Great Expectations*, when Pip takes the stolen pork pie to Magwitch in the marshes, it has been hand-made by Mrs Pip. Severe that hand may be when the 'Tickler' is in it, but her pies are pure. So hungry is Magwitch, though, he would probably have been as happy with one of Mr Brooks's feline confections.

ஊ Piplick ஒ

E.M. Forster observes in *Aspects of the Novel* that there are two kinds of novelist: those who create flat characters and those who create round characters. Dickens, Forster goes on to tell us, is the grandmaster of flat characterisation. It's a variation on Orwell's similarly well-known observation that Dickens's comic characters are incarcerated in their own single, salient characteristic. Pumblechook is always Pumblechookian, Micawber is always Micawberish, Podsnap ditto.

Forster's remark about Dickens's flat characters has become a much iterated critical 'truth'. If I had a pound for every time I've

read it in a student essay my pension pot would be twice the size
it is.

One can, and should, complicate Forster's over-simple gener-
alisation. Dickens's flat characterisation can be argued to be analo-
gous to what Picasso does when he shows two sides of the same
face on the same plane. Looked at carefully there is something
interestingly Picasso-prismatic, and artfully duplicitous, about
Dickensian characterisation.

Principally this complexity originates in the narrative oddity
that the villains are, very often, in a Mr Hyde relationship with
the heroes. The simplest example is in *A Tale of Two Cities*. Sydney
Carton and Charles Darnay are, one could plausibly argue, the
same young man viewed from different angles.

Pip, that sanctified youngster of *Great Expectations*, fantasises
at one point about bashing Mrs Joe's head in. Who actually per-
petrates that brain-damaging assault? The churlish blacksmith
Dolge Orlick. David Copperfield, we plausibly suppose, is sexually
attracted to Little Em'ly. But he cannot, of course, marry a working-
class girl and he is too inherently decent to take advantage of her.
Who seduces and abandons Emily? David's alter ego, Steerforth.

One can, with a little critical slack, assimilate these six into the
double-single characters: Piplick, Copperforth, Cartnay. One is
encouraged to play this mix-and-match game by the erotic merg-
ing that occurs at key moments in the narratives. When Orlick
has lured Pip down to the deserted lime-kiln in the marshes, what
reader will not pick up the sexual resonance in his assault?

'Now,' said a suppressed voice with an oath, 'I've got you!'
   'What is this?' I cried, struggling. 'Who is it? Help, help, help!'
   Not only were my arms pulled close to my sides, but the
pressure on my bad arm caused me exquisite pain. Sometimes,

a strong man's hand, sometimes a strong man's breast, was set against my mouth to deaden my cries, and with a hot breath always close to me, I struggled ineffectually in the dark, while I was fastened tight to the wall. 'And now,' said the suppressed voice with another oath, 'call out again, and I'll make short work of you!'

What work? Hot breath? Exquisite pain?

Pip at the lime-kiln.

When he looks down on the corpse of the drowned Steerforth, David uses the language of a lover:

> I was up with the dull dawn, and, having dressed as quietly as I could, looked into his room. He was fast asleep; lying, easily, with his head upon his arm, as I had often seen him lie at school.

When he was sneaking from the older boy's room, hastily dressed, at dull dawn, perhaps.

∽ Poetryless ∾

'Dickens and Poetry' would comprise a very anaemic book. Dickens admired verse sufficiently to name two of his sons after leading poets, Walter Landor and Alfred Lord Tennyson. But unlike Thackeray, George Eliot, or Hardy he has no body of verse to his own name. None of his characters are poets or poetically inclined. Nor do his principal characters seem to draw nourishment from poetry.

Dickens's prejudice against poetry as something vitally important to his time seems to centre on the belief that it does not engage, as does the kind of fiction he practised, with real-world issues. The nearest thing to a poet in the novels is Skimpole in *Bleak House*. He is also one of Dickens's most mercilessly satirised characters. Skimpole is based, as everyone at the time recognised, on Leigh Hunt – a poet, and a patron of greater poets than himself (Shelley and Keats, notably).

Skimpole is given to such utterances as:

> 'Take an extreme case. Take the case of the slaves on American plantations. I dare say they are worked hard, I dare say they don't

Skimpole being Skimpole.

altogether like it. I dare say theirs is an unpleasant experience on the whole; but they people the landscape for me, they give it a poetry for me, and perhaps that is one of the pleasanter objects of their existence. I am very sensible of it, if it be, and I shouldn't wonder if it were!'

Poets, that is, regard the world as something to contemplate for their own onanistic enjoyment, not as something to change for the good of humanity. Poetry is, essentially, a *selfish* art form. A hundred years later W.H. Auden would concede that his poems saved not a single Jew from the gas chamber. Dickens would have agreed, one feels.

Bleak House was published 1852–53. The book everyone in England and America was reading (more so than even Boz's latest) was Harriet Beecher Stowe's anti-slavery novel, *Uncle Tom's Cabin*. Dickens is clearly alluding to it in Skimpole's effusion. (He is also satirising what he saw as silliness in Leigh Hunt's autobiography, published in 1850. His last published work, his literary powers long since enfeebled, it is as vapid and self-regarding a volume as Dickens's spiteful depiction of Skimpole suggests.)

Abraham Lincoln, it is alleged, took Harriet Beecher Stowe's hand and saluted her as the author of a little book that had started a great war. No mere poem could change history. Novels could. Dickens also shook Mrs Stowe's hand, when – as the author of the day – she visited England in 1853. He privately recorded finding her 'silly' and 'moony'. Perhaps her sales figures prejudiced him.

Does Dickens, one wonders, lie uneasy in Poets' Corner?

༄ Pubs ༄

In the darkest days of his childhood – when he was put to work in the blacking factory – Dickens confided to John Forster one bright spot:

> I remember, one evening … that I went into a public-house in Parliament-street, which is still there though altered, at the corner of the short street leading into Cannon Row, and said to the landlord behind the bar, 'What is your very best – the VERY *best* – ale, a glass?' For, the occasion was a festive one, for some reason: I forget why. It may have been my birthday, or somebody else's. 'Twopence,' says he. 'Then,' says I, 'just draw me a glass of that, if you please, with a good head to it.' The landlord

looked at me, in return, over the bar, from head to foot, with a strange smile on his face; and instead of drawing the beer, looked round the screen and said something to his wife, who came out from behind it, with her work in her hand, and joined him in surveying me. Here we stand, all three, before me now, in my study in Devonshire Terrace. The landlord, in his shirt-sleeves, leaning against the bar window-frame; his wife, looking over the little half-door; and I, in some confusion, looking up at them from outside the partition. They asked me a good many questions, as what my name was, how old I was, where I lived, how I was employed, etc. To all of which, that I might commit nobody, I invented appropriate answers. They served me with the ale, though I suspect it was not the strongest on the premises; and the landlord's wife, opening the little half-door and bending down gave me a kiss that was half-admiring and half-compassionate, but all womanly and good, I am sure.

This event is reproduced, word for word, in *David Copperfield*, Chapter 11, where the young hero receives from the publican's wife a maternal kindness he has never hitherto known since his mother was driven to an early grave by the Murdstones.

Dickens retained a warm place in his heart for the British pub all his life. That warm feeling was reciprocated. Google 'Dickensian pubs' and you will be offered a choice of thirst-quenching crawls. There is no blue plaque, but The Betsey Trotwood in Farringdon Road commemorates where David Copperfield's adoptive mother had her cottage. Routes feature such other hostelries as The Cheshire Cheese in Fleet Street (said to be the author's favourite pub) and The Bleeding Heart in Clerkenwell, prominent in *Little Dorrit*.

On the whole Dickens preferred cosy boozers to the more up-market coaching houses that snootily called themselves 'inns',

David orders his glass of ale.

offering accommodation and restaurant-standard catering rather than pub grub. The Jolly Bargemen in *Great Expectations* (where Joe Gargery has his nightly three pints) is much more inviting than The Blue Boar (where, once he's a gent, Pip prefers to lodge when in town). An exception is The Angel coaching house, in Bury St Edmunds, which still trades on its key episode in *The Pickwick Papers*. *Pickwick* also boasts the pub most referenced in his fiction, The George and Vulture in the City, near Lombard Street. There are some twenty mentions.

Thackeray, Dickens's great rival, was a clubman, not a pubman. But, of course, the author of *Vanity Fair* was public-school. Public houses were for a lower kind of English gentleman. Like the author of *David Copperfield*.

୶ Punishment ୬

Michel Foucault's *Discipline and Punish* (1975) is a critical book that has been hugely influential in my professional lifetime. The thesis is simple. Until the early nineteenth century penal systems addressed the body of the guilty person. Prison reform replaced corporal punishment with systems that addressed the mind of the guilty person.

Lex talionis (eyes for eyes) gave way to moral rehabilitation. But in both systems, Foucault argues, it was the exercise of authoritarian power that was at their centre. A boot stamping on a human face for ever – as Winston Smith is told by O'Brien in *Nineteen Eighty-four*. Sometimes the boot looks different. That's all.

Foucault's book opens with a description of the public execution of Robert-François Damiens for the 'parricidal' crime of an attempt on the life of Louis XV. The atrocity was something that had stuck in Dickens's mind ever since he trembled at the account of it in the *Terrific Register*, aged twelve (a period when he was anything but kindly inclined towards his own father).

He introduces it at length in *A Tale of Two Cities*, where a 'countryman' speculates about what awaits Gaspard for the murder of 'Monseigneur':

> [H]is right hand, armed with the knife, will be burnt off before his face; that, into wounds which will be made in his arms, his breast, and his legs, there will be poured boiling oil, melted lead, hot resin, wax, and sulphur; finally, that he will be torn limb from limb by four strong horses. That old man says, all this was actually done to a prisoner who made an attempt on the life of the late King, Louis Fifteen.

It was indeed 'actually done', he is told. 'The name of that prisoner was Damiens.'

Dickens believed in capital punishment – particularly after the Indian Mutiny, when his attitude approximates to that of Kurtz in *Heart of Darkness* – 'exterminate the brutes'. But he was against the contemporary brutalities of the cat-o'-nine-tails, the treadmill, and oakum-picking in British prisons.

He was, equally (and rather paradoxically) against the newfangled 'separate and silent' system – keeping prisoners in specially constructed penitentiaries, under constant 'panoptical' surveillance. The experiment was brought to its highest pitch in mid-century prisons in London's Pentonville and in Philadelphia.

Dickens's objection to the 'separate and silent' system was two-pronged. The humane Dickens believed that it could drive a prisoner mad. This is expressed in Dr Manette ('105 North Tower') in *A Tale of Two Cities*, who becomes in his Bastille isolation a

Dr Manette in the Bastille.

catatonic corpse, tapping away on his shoemaker's last. The sterner Dickens believed that the 'separate and silent' system might, paradoxically, go too easy on malefactors.

Conditions in Pentonville's single-occupancy cells were 'humane': comfortable bunks, wash-basins, toilet facilities, warmth, good food. It was all too much for Dickens, who satirised the treatment of these 'pet prisoners' in his journalism and in the depiction of Prisoner 27 (formerly known as Uriah Heep) and Prisoner 28 (formerly known as Littimer) in *David Copperfield*.

Both are gaming the Pentonville system brilliantly:

'Twenty Eight,' said a gentleman in spectacles, who had not yet
spoken, 'you complained last week, my good fellow, of the cocoa.
How has it been since?'
　'I thank you, sir,' said Mr Littimer, 'it has been better made.
If I might take the liberty of saying so, sir, I don't think the milk
which is boiled with it is quite genuine ...'

Both he and No 27 are, they assure the prison visitors, 'reformed
characters'. Humbug.

✺ Rats ✺

Like many people who have spent formative years in slum housing,
Dickens had a prejudice against rats. With him, in fact, it amounted
to outright terror. As with Winston Smith, Dickens's Room 101
could well have featured a rat, scrabbling to get at his eyeballs.
　Like Orwell's hero, Dickens's aversion was based on the fact
that rats – as Victorian London portrayed as clearly as any 1914–18
battlefield – ate human flesh. In *Bleak House*, as he conducts Lady
Dedlock to the graveyard ('what a scene of horror!') where Nemo
is buried, Jo yelps out excitedly: 'Look at the rat! ... Hi, Look!
There he goes! Ho! Into the ground.' His belly full of the luckless
Nemo, doubtless.
　Dickens's rodentophobia was instilled at an early age. In *The
Uncommercial Traveller*, which he published at the late age of 48,
he recalls the horrific tales his nurse told him 40 years before, as a
child in Chatham. Most horrible was that of 'Chips', a shipwright
who makes a pact with the devil in return for 'an iron pot and a

bushel of tenpenny nails and half a ton of copper and a rat that could speak'.

The metal is useful but Chips decides he can do without the talkative rat, and tries to kill the animal by throwing it into a cauldron of boiling pitch. The rat, undamaged, pops right out – with an ominous leer. The next day, Chips

> put his rule into the long pocket at the side of his trousers, and there he found a rat – not that rat, but another rat. And in his hat, he found another; and in his pocket-handkerchief, another; and in the sleeves of his coat, when he pulled it on to go to dinner, two more.

To cut a very long story short, he soon has more rats than a dog has fleas, before the Great Rat himself returns to devour him. Horribly.

As Dickens recalls, for the whole of his life, he has been morbidly afraid of 'my own pocket, lest my exploring hand should find a specimen or two of those vermin in it'. It was a later horror in the blacking factory, where he was sent to work as a child, that it was 'swarming with rats'.

Harry Stone makes the convincing argument that rats,

> especially subterranean rats, rats in the dark depths, were … a quintessential, and quintessentially loathsome, embodiment for Dickens of hell, aggressive malignancy, cannibalism, and early childhood trauma.

Put more simply, they frightened the life out of him.

Londoners are routinely informed that, although they may not know it, they are never more than a hundred feet away from a rat. Dickens was, lifelong, much closer than that.

↜ **Ravens** ↝

Of all birds Dickens loved ravens most. He was, said one of his friends, 'raven-mad'. Over the years he kept two in his house, both named 'Grip' (from their habit of gripping on to the shoulder of their owner to perch). The birds are famously intelligent. They can mimic human speech as well as parrots and have been taught to count and do amazing tricks.

Why Dickens kept them as household pets is not clear. Perhaps, with memory of Proverbs 30:17, it was to keep his errant children in line: 'The eye that mocketh at his father, and despiseth to obey his mother, the ravens of the valley shall pick it out.' Or perhaps it was the good press they get elsewhere in the Bible. The raven is the first bird Noah sends out from the ark, and ravens feed Elijah in his hour of need.

Grip gets a good press also in *Barnaby Rudge*. In Chapter 57, as the sainted idiot gets caught up in the Gordon Riots, his bird steals the show,

> crying, as he sidled up to his master, 'I'm a devil, I'm a Polly, I'm a kettle, I'm a Protestant, No Popery!' Having learnt this latter sentiment from the gentry among whom he had lived of late, he delivered it with uncommon emphasis.
>
> 'Well said, Grip!' cried his master, as he fed him with the daintiest bits. 'Well said, old boy!'
>
> 'Never say die, bow wow wow, keep up your spirits, Grip Grip Grip, Holloa! We'll all have tea, I'm a Protestant kettle, No Popery!' cried the raven.
>
> 'Gordon for ever, Grip!' cried Barnaby.

Dickens's novel was reviewed, enthusiastically, by Edgar Allan Poe in Philadelphia in 1842. Poe had just one reservation:

> The raven … intensely amusing as it is, might have been made, more than we now see it, a portion of the conception of the fantastic Barnaby. Its croakings might have been *prophetically* heard in the course of the drama.

Two years later Poe went on to create his own talking, prophesying Grip ('Nevermore') in his most famous poem, 'The Raven'.

Dickens had the Grip who kept him company while he was writing *Barnaby Rudge* preserved with arsenic, stuffed and put in a glass case. The luckless bird had died after pecking lead-based paint on the walls of the Dickens house at 1 Devonshire Terrace. The bird is since 1971 in the possession of the Philadelphia Free Library.

There is no blue plaque for Grip at Devonshire Terrace, alas (nor, any more, for Dickens, since the house was pulled down). Poe's poem is perhaps memorial enough.

❧ Resurrection ☙

Dickens was fascinated (and horrified) by the line in the Eucharist:

> Then Jesus said to them … 'I am the living bread which came down from heaven. If any man eat of this bread, he shall live for ever; and the bread that I will give, is My Flesh, for the life of the world.'

There follows the promise of resurrection.

Christianity, a Martian might think, is based on cannibalism ('give us this day our daily Jesus') and worship of a corpse that will, miraculously, come back to life not as a spirit but in the original wholly undecayed flesh.

Dickens's intense curiosity about these central 'cannibal and corpse' mysteries of his faith is reflected in his fiction (*see* 'Cannibalism'). Miss Havisham in *Great Expectations*, for example, stopped her life at a sacramental moment – her wedding day, and at the precise moment the wedding breakfast was to be celebrated with communion.

On his second visit to Satis House (Chapter 11) she conducts Pip, her 'withered hand round his', to a sealed, candle-lit room. At its centre is a table, and at the centre of the table, a something

> so heavily overhung with cobwebs that its form was quite undis-tinguishable; and, as I looked along the yellow expanse out of which I remember its seeming to grow, like a black fungus, I saw speckled-legged spiders with blotchy bodies running home to it, and running out from it ...

The decayed thing is a cake, she explains. 'A bride-cake. Mine!' Miss Havisham then summons her relatives – all greedy to inherit her wealth. She pokes, with her stick, where they must sit 'when I am laid on that table' – alongside the cake. 'Now you all know where to take your stations when you come to feast upon me.'

It's an odd and wholly blasphemous parody of the Eucharist. The cake is the wafer, her body will lie on the altar (the word 'table' is used by low churches) and, transubstantiated, her flesh will be consumed by her worshippers.

In *A Tale of Two Cities* the resurrection theme is what, over many such scenes, binds the novel into a whole. Dr Manette is 'brought back to life' from interment in the Bastille (a cave of sorts). Jerry Cruncher, a criminal resurrectionist (so called) by trade, digs up corpses for the anatomist: once dismembered, how will those bodies ever be resurrected whole?

The novel ends with a pseudo-crucifixion and the 'It is a far, far better thing' monologue. Sydney Carton does not die. He is resurrected, of course, in his other body: that of Charles Darnay, for whom he is guillotined.

Did Dickens believe in resurrection? Probably no more than he believed in revolution. But both fascinated him.

∽ Sausages ∾

The first entry of a sausage into the plot of a Dickens novel is in *Oliver Twist*, when the hero makes his entry into Fagin's thieves' kitchen. It is, as the fish-and-chip shops say, 'frying tonight':

> The walls and ceiling of the room were perfectly black with age and dirt. There was a deal table before the fire: upon which were a candle, stuck in a ginger-beer bottle, two or three pewter pots, a loaf and butter, and a plate. In a frying-pan, which was on the fire, and which was secured to the mantelshelf by a string, some sausages were cooking; and standing over them, with a toasting-fork in his hand, was a very old shrivelled Jew, whose villainous-looking and repulsive face was obscured by a quantity of matted red hair.

There is complex allusion here. Red hair is traditionally associated with Judas, betrayer of Christ (how, incidentally, does the unworldly Oliver know, without being told, that Fagin is Jewish?).

George Cruikshank

Fagin cooks.

Sausages are invariably pork in Dickens. Fagin is not just a Jew, but a bad Jew. He is elsewhere described as the 'merry old gentle-man' – a proverbial phrase for the devil. The brandished toasting fork recalls the instrument the evil one uses to toss around those poor souls roasting in hell. Fagin, we apprehend, is a diabolic, Christ-betraying, bad Jew. Rarely has a sausage been so expressive.

Sausages figure, relatively unimportantly, elsewhere in the fiction. In *Little Dorrit* the murderer Rigaud calls in a superior Lyons sausage in prison, wrapped in a vine leaf. It is, of course, a French prison.

Most charmingly, in his first visit to Wemmick's 'castle' in the Walworth Road in *Great Expectations*, Pip is somewhat put off his food by the propinquity of the family pig a few feet away in the yard. On his second visit, the pig is even nearer – on the table as sausages – and now is entirely welcome. 'In all respects a first-rater', as Wemmick proudly observes.

✄ Secrets ✄

The Victorians – even Mrs Grundy herself – never covered up piano legs. Their sexual practices, however, they did keep from prying eyes. The classic study of the Victorian sexual underworld is an eleven-volume chronicle of a sexual athlete's progress (he claims a lifelong score of 1,200 partners) entitled *My Secret Life*. It was published (prudently abroad) in the mid-1880s. The author is known to posterity only as 'Walter' (he was probably the bibliophile, Henry Spencer Ashbee – Dickens quite likely knew him to say hello to).

The Victorians were genius at keeping their secret lives secret. What, then, about Dickens's? One can begin with his most autobiographical hero, Pip in *Great Expectations* – the character he created at the period (1859–61) when he incinerated all his private papers, separated from Mrs Dickens, caught venereal disease, and was in total personal turmoil.

Is the 30-year-old Pip, in that last scene with Estella in the ruined garden at Satis House, as virginal as he was when we first encountered him as a seven-year-old in the graveyard? Hints buried deep in the text suggest that Pip may not have kept the temple of his body entirely pure.

When, for example, Herbert Pocket warns 'DO NOT GO HOME', Pip spends the night in a private room at the Hummums (Turkish baths). The place is evidently well known to him. He has terrible nightmares about spiders. There were other unsavoury clients. Then, as now, the bath house was the place of 'assignation': where a young man could enjoy illicit pleasures of the night (with either sex).

One of the most tantalising pullings aside of the Dickensian curtain in the recently (2009) completed edition of his letters is a coded communication by Dickens to his personal physician, Frank Beard, at around this same fraught period. He writes, on 8 July 1859, that he is troubled by a 'small malady', caused by his 'bachelor state'. The biographer Michael Slater notes that it was 'apparently venereal'. Claire Tomalin, picking up a joking comment in a letter to Wilkie Collins, deduces a dose of gonorrhoea.

The problem was certainly not erectile dysfunction. Mrs Dickens, when he was in his marital state, bore him ten children. The last was born in 1852 (at this period, one suspects, sexual relations were suspended). He did not, the evidence suggests, install Ellen Ternan as his mistress until a little later in the 1860s. In the intervals, quite likely, he took his pleasures more randomly at places like the Hummums. More we shall never probably know. His secret life is secret.

Do we think less of Dickens for his (presumed) incontinence? His female readers would have done. Modern biographers tend to shrug it off broad-mindedly. He was a man of the world – the Victorian world.

∽ Serialisation ∾

The new novel, by a top-rated novelist, was hugely expensive in Victorian Britain. Ever since Walter Scott pioneered the form, it came in three volumes and cost a whopping 31 shillings and six-pence (around £60 today). One way round the high cost was the 'circulating library' system, which came into its own in the 1840s and 1850s. It suited the libraries to maintain the 'three-decker' (i.e. three-volume) form, because more than one customer could be catered for with one novel.

Dickens disliked the three-decker because it created barriers (notably censorious librarians) between himself and his reader-ship. He wanted intimate contact. Serialisation was one way of achieving it. Every one of Dickens's major novels was serialised.

With *The Pickwick Papers*, in collaboration with his publishers Chapman & Hall Dickens pioneered the monthly serial. It cost a shilling an instalment, which comprised 32 pages with two full-page illustrations. There would be twenty instalments, the last a 'double' costing two shillings. There would also be a follow-up multi-volume version of the novel. Thus published, a novel like *Pickwick* was not cheap in its serial parts – it still cost a pound – but the cost was spread over a year and a half.

Serialisation was a crucial factor in composition. The writer, like Dickens (who became a master in it), was writing to 'two unities' – that of the part, and that of the whole. Since the novel had to be sold nineteen times, strategies to keep the reader 'on the hook' were vital: suspense, excitement, mystery, pathos, climax. As Wilkie Collins put it, the art of the serialist could be summed up as: 'make 'em laugh, make 'em cry, make 'em wait'.

During the late 1850s and 1860s the monthly 'novel in parts' gave way to the serial in monthly and weekly magazines. These were cheaper and offered a miscellany of surrounding items. Dickens was virtuosic in both dimensions.

The reader who bears in mind the two architectures (serial part/three volumes) has an enriched experience. The second weekly instalment of *Great Expectations*, for example (it would have come out just before Christmas), concludes with the constable arriving to interrupt the Gargerys' Christmas party. He pushes a pair of handcuffs at Pip, who is harrowed with guilt at having helped the convict Magwitch (boys were hanged in England at that date for doing that kind of thing). The reader had to wait a whole week to discover that this agent of the law merely wants the cuffs mended by Joe, the blacksmith.

The first volume of the follow-up three-volume edition of *Great Expectations* ends on Chapter 19, with Pip leaving his country home for the great city. Christian and the Celestial City in *The Pilgrim's Progress* are evoked.

> We changed [stagecoach horses] again and yet again, and it was now too late and too far to go back, and I went on. And the mists had all solemnly risen now, and the world lay spread before me.

Imagine the suspense, having to wait until you could borrow the next volume from the library, to find out how Pip, with his great expectations, will fare in London.

✍ Smells ✍

Norman Mailer once complained that there is not a single smell in Hemingway. There are plenty in Dickens – stinks, aromas, fragrances; the whole range of nose experience. He can be positively virtuosic on the topic, as in the following delightful passage in *Martin Chuzzlewit*:

> Many and many a pleasant stroll they had in Covent Garden Market; snuffing up the perfume of the fruits and flowers, wondering at the magnificence of the pineapples and melons; catching glimpses down side avenues, of rows and rows of old women, seated on inverted baskets, shelling peas; looking unutterable things at the fat bundles of asparagus with which the dainty shops were fortified as with a breastwork; and, at the herbalist's doors, gratefully inhaling scents as of veal-stuffing yet uncooked, dreamily mixed up with capsicums, brown-paper, seeds, even with hints of lusty snails and fine young curly leeches.

Every Dickens novel has a range of smells, but usually one is distinctive and as powerful as Proust's madeleine.

What are the distinctive smells of the following?

1. *Bleak House*
2. *Our Mutual Friend*
3. *Edwin Drood*
4. *Oliver Twist*
5. *Great Expectations*

Bleak House? – the pea-souper. *Our Mutual Friend*? – two smells: the putrid Thames ('Old Stinks') and the equally unfragrant dust heaps. *Edwin Drood*? – the fumes of the opium den in the first chapter permeate the whole novel. *Oliver Twist*? – those frying sausages, sweat and candle fumes that assault the young hero's nostrils as he enters Fagin's den (*see* 'Sausages'). *Great Expectations*? – the acrid smell of the white-hot forge fire; the sharper smell of charred wood after a house fire; and the more bitter smell of burning lime from the kilns on the marsh. Pumblechook's grain shop supplies the odd whiff.

Some future Kindle may be able to aromatise the texts we read. Dickens will profit more than most writers – certainly more than Hemingway.

✑ Spontaneous Combustion ✑

The tenth number of *Bleak House* (December 1852) has, by way of Christmas present, what Victorians called a 'tremendous scene' – the 'spontaneous combustion' of the rag and bone merchant Krook:

> Here is a small burnt patch of flooring; here is the tinder from a little bundle of burnt paper, but not so light as usual, seeming to be steeped in something; and here is – is it the cinder of a small charred and broken log of wood sprinkled with white ashes, or is it coal? Oh, horror, he IS here! And this from which we run away, striking out the light and overturning one another into the street, is all that represents him … Call the death by any name your Highness will, attribute it to whom you will, or say it might have been prevented how you will, it is the same death eternally – inborn, inbred, engendered in the corrupted humours of the vicious body itself, and that only – spontaneous combustion, and none other of all the deaths that can be died.

Famously, the spontaneous combustion episode landed Dickens in controversy. Reviewing the novel as it was appearing serially,

G.H. Lewes (George Eliot's consort) remarked that the explosion of Krook as a consequence of over-indulgence in gin was scientifically nonsensical. London's 'Gin Lane' was not a bomb site. A violent interchange of polemic between the two men of letters – both arguing their corners by reference to 'science' (in which Lewes was by far the better informed) – ensued. The dispute rumbled on for months, with Dickens getting distinctly the worst of it.

With hindsight, and 150 years of literary criticism, the modern reader can easily resolve the controversy. With 'spontaneous combustion' Dickens was creating a metaphor for the *socially* explosive consequences of the social evils (notably the corrupt legal system) that the novel elsewhere addresses. But Dickens always regarded himself as a realist – not a poet. Anything that seemed to question the literal 'truth' of his writing was anathema to him.

Although at the time Lewes won game, set and match, Dickens turned out to be right, in a way. In America, in the 1980s, authorities were baffled by bodies that were found, reduced to small piles of ash, with no plausible explanation. Forensic research discovered that if someone – usually paralytic drunk and smoking – fell into comatose sleep, the blanket could smoulder and the effect of heat on the sleeper would release enough body fat to produce a 'candlewick effect'. It was entered into the medical textbooks as 'spontaneous combustion'.

Somewhere the ghost of Dickens must have chortled. He loved being right.

✃ Streaky Bacon ✄

Consider the following famous speech in *Great Expectations*. Magwitch has just grabbed Pip and is intending to terrorise him

into bringing him food and the wherewithal to file off his mana-
cles (it's psychologically wholly unconvincing – not one in a million little boys would ever put a foot back into those marshes: for
as long as they lived, some of them).

Magwitch clinches his instructions with a gothic threat:

'Now, I ain't alone, as you may think I am. There's a young
man hid with me, in comparison with which young man I am
a Angel. That young man hears the words I speak. That young
man has a secret way pecooliar to himself, of getting at a boy,
and at his heart, and at his liver. It is in wain for a boy to attempt
to hide himself from that young man. A boy may lock his door,
may be warm in bed, may tuck himself up, may draw the clothes
over his head, may think himself comfortable and safe, but that
young man will softly creep and creep his way to him and tear
him open. I am a-keeping that young man from harming of you
at the present moment, with great difficulty. I find it wery hard
to hold that young man off of your inside.'

It's pure, double-distilled essence of Dickens. But how to define
what makes this the kind of passage that, as Coleridge said of
Wordsworth, if you saw it wandering wild in Arabia, you would
shout out 'Boz!'

There is a wholly idiosyncratic mix of fun and horror. I have
a friend who, when he's drunk, leans into my (glumly sober)
face and recites Magwitch's words about the young man. He does
so in a spirit of high hilarity (after the thirtieth time, it's a bit
wearing). But what is funny about having your liver torn out and
devoured?

Unsurprisingly, it was Dickens himself who came up with
exactly the right term for this peculiarly Dickensian effect. 'Streaky

bacon' he called it in *Oliver Twist* (Chapter 17), where he wrote:

> It is the custom on the stage, in all good murderous melodra-
> mas, to present the tragic and the comic scenes, in as regular
> alternation, as the layers of red and white in a side of streaky
> bacon.

A lifelong lover of the theatre (his first hope in life was to be an
actor not a novelist), Dickens employed the streaky bacon effect
brilliantly in his fiction.

✧ Street-Sweepings ✧

Jo, in *Bleak House*, is a crossing-sweeper. But what, precisely,
does he sweep? The Victorians knew an awful lot better than
we do.

The simplest answer is 'mud'. Dickens launches into a rhapsody
on the substance in the opening paragraph of *Bleak House*:

> London. Michaelmas term lately over, and the Lord Chancellor
> sitting in Lincoln's Inn Hall. Implacable November weather. As
> much mud in the streets as if the waters had but newly retired
> from the face of the earth …

Here Dickens playfully pictures mud as the relatively pure primal
soup from which the post-diluvian world has evolved. But 'mud'
throws back an unplayful echo, *merde* – shit. *Merde* was elsewhere
compounded into two of the author's most biting names: Merdle
(in *Little Dorrit*) and Murdstone (in *David Copperfield*). Shitty
characters both of them.

Young street-sweepers.

What, specifically, was London mud? Norman Gash analyses its content, fingers on nose, in *Robert Surtees and Early Victorian Society*:

Everyone agreed that London was the dirtiest of English cities. The central streets were covered with a thick layer of filth, the principal ingredients of which were horse manure, stone-dust from the constant grinding of iron tyres on the paving stones, and soot descending from the forest of London chimneys. The resultant compound resembled a black paste, which clung glutinously to everything it touched and emitted a characteristic odour reminiscent of a cattle market ... London produced such a vast amount of excrement, both animal and human, that the surrounding agricultural districts were unable to absorb it. As a result the streets seemed to remain permanently foul. To get across busy streets, especially in wet weather, was a hazardous business except at the regular paths – 'isthmuses of comparative dry land', as one observer called them – kept clean by the unremitting work of crossing sweepers.

As much any Londoner of the time, Jo the Sweeper earned his pennies – and even the half-crowns that the kinder-hearted Snagsby slipped his way.

৵৹ Svengali ৶৵

Dickens first became interested in hypnotism in the 1830s, at exactly the same period that he became a novelist. It was at the height of the 'mesmeric mania'. Dickens had been introduced to the new science by its arch apostle, Dr John Elliotson. Elliotson foresaw a great therapeutic future for hypnosis – principally as an anaesthetic (chloroform was still ten years away).

Dickens attended Elliotson's demonstrations at the University of London, where (until he was dismissed by the university's less infatuated governors) the doctor was employed and from whose lecture platform he evangelised about hypnosis.

Mesmerism intrudes into Dickens's novels in scenes such as that where, in a trance, Oliver Twist 'sees' Monks and Sikes at his window in the Brownlow house. They are not, of course, there. Elliotson liked to show with his prize exhibits how, under the influence, a person could see things miles away – 'mental travelling', it was called.

Dickens allowed himself to be mesmerised to counteract his chronic insomnia; and, never one to be passive, learned the procedure himself. He was soon adept at sending Mrs Dickens to sleep.

Kate, however, was less pleased with her husband's greatest experiment in the hypnotic art. On their trip to Italy in 1844–45 he fell in with what Michael Slater describes as the 'petite English wife of a Swiss banker resident in Genoa called Emile de la Rue'.

It might be truer to say he 'fell in love', and he found an ingenious way of prosecuting the affair.

Augusta de la Rue suffered 'from an acute neurasthenic disorder which caused spectral illusions, convulsions, even catalepsy at times'. Confident he could cure her with his mesmeric powers, Dickens embarked on an intense, months-long relationship with her. On one occasion, as Slater delicately records:

> He was summoned to the de la Rues' bedroom one night to find Madame 'rolled into an apparently impossible ball, by tic in the brain' and was only able to find where her head was, 'by following her long hair to its source'.

Catherine, pregnant as always, is described as 'very uneasy'. Well she might be.

At the end of his life Dickens diverted his flagging, but still formidable energies away from journalism and fiction to public readings of his work. There were a number of motives. Money obviously. But also the 'influence' that he could exercise over his audience. It was not hypnosis, it was mass hypnosis. Commentators have called it the 'Svengali effect' after George du Maurier's evil hypnotist. How much Dickens would have liked being associated with a lesser novelist (as he would certainly have considered du Maurier) is a moot point.

৶ Teeth ৸

There is, amazingly, no portrait, photograph, or sketch of Anthony Trollope extant, until a couple that were done shortly before his death (he looks in them like 'death warmed up').

There are quite a few representations of Thackeray (most beautifully the Boehm statuette, now in the Garrick Club) but nowhere near as many as there are of Dickens, whose narcissism is memorialised in innumerable depictions by lens, brush, and pencil.

It is fascinating to review them in sequence (Google Images is helpful), watching, year by year, the hair on the scalp recede, and the hair on the chin advance. Beautiful in youth, Dickens was imposing in age. But in all those scores of representations we never see his teeth.

This is not unusual. Promiscuous display of one's teeth was very bad form in respectable Victorian society. It was associated with brutes like Bill Sikes in *Oliver Twist* ('"Wolves tear your throats!" muttered Sikes, grinding his teeth') and villains like James Carker in *Dombey and Son*:

> Mr Carker was a gentleman thirty-eight or forty years old, of a florid complexion, and with two unbroken rows of glistening teeth, whose regularity and whiteness were quite distressing. It was impossible to escape the observation of them, for he showed them whenever he spoke; and bore so wide a smile upon his countenance (a smile, however, very rarely, indeed, extending beyond his mouth), that there was something in it like the snarl of a cat.

Enough said. Those snappers say it all.

Victorian dentophobia is routinely ascribed to rotten or non-existent teeth, or the age's lamentably imperfect false teeth. In fact, Dickens seems to have looked after what was in his mouth rather carefully and to have taken a reasonably good mouthful with him under the stone in Poets' Corner. As Claire Tomalin records, he had a dental plate that was giving him trouble towards the end

Mr Carker smiles toothily.

of his life. In 2010, his ivory-handled toothpick came up for auction in New York. Victorians generally preferred picks to brushes – and when they did brush, often used soot instead of toothpaste. According to an accompanying letter by his sister-in-law and housekeeper, he used the pick 'on his last visit to America' and up to his death in 1870. It had a retracting point and the handle was inlaid with gold.

The toothpick fetched $9,150 – well over its reserve. Whether the new owner dared clean his teeth with it is not recorded.

᧞ Thames (1. Death and Rebirth) ᧞

The Thames runs centrally through Dickens's fiction, as it does through the place where almost all of his fiction is set – London. The great river has three personalities for Dickens. It is the source of rebirth. It is a place of death. It is a stream of corruption.

The Thames is tidal at London – it sweeps in as clean water, and ebbs as unclean water. It is both baptismal and sanitary. For Dickens it is the place where the mysterious process of drowning into life happens (as it does in Shakespeare's *The Tempest*). There is no finer description of drowning anywhere, I think, than John Harmon's in the Thames in *Our Mutual Friend*. But it is also as much a rebirth as Ferdinand's in *The Tempest*:

'It was only after a downward slide through something like a tube, and then a great noise and a sparkling and crackling as of fires, that the consciousness came upon me, "This is John Harmon drowning! John Harmon, struggle for your life. John Harmon, call on Heaven and save yourself!" I think I cried it out aloud in a great agony, and then a heavy horrid unintelligible something vanished, and it was I who was struggling there alone in the water.

'I was very weak and faint, frightfully oppressed with drowsiness, and driving fast with the tide. Looking over the black water, I saw the lights racing past me on the two banks of the river, as if they were eager to be gone and leave me dying in the dark. The tide was running down, but I knew nothing of up or down then. When, guiding myself safely with Heaven's assistance before the fierce set of the water, I at last caught at a boat moored, one of a tier of boats at a causeway, I was sucked under her, and came up, only just alive, on the other side.'

The tube is the womb through which he travels to his new existence. He emerges from the water a newborn man, John Rokesmith.

The drowning and rebirth is a metaphor for what all human beings go through, as they progress morally and spiritually in life. It is also a metaphor for the river's complex and purifying

Watery death.

relationship with the sinful city. It was the Thames, we recall, that ran past the blacking factory where Dickens worked as a child, every day taking young Charles's burden of misery with it – until the next morning.

ᥥ Thames (2. Pauper's Graveyard) ᥬ

One of the few poems that one knows Dickens to have loved is Thomas Hood's 'Bridge of Sighs':

> ONE more Unfortunate,
>   Weary of breath,
> Rashly importunate,
>   Gone to her death!
>
> Take her up tenderly,
>   Lift her with care;
> Fashion'd so slenderly
>   Young, and so fair!

Gaffer Hexam, fisher for corpses in *Our Mutual Friend*, is anything but tender taking up his morning's catch of those who cast themselves into the Thames the night before. He goes through his haul with the eye of an expert angler (the gaff, we recall, is the cruel hook that anglers insert into the gills of their fish, to lift them out of the water):

> 'This one was the young woman in grey boots, and her linen marked with a cross. Look and see if she warn't.'
>   'Quite right.'

'This is him as had a nasty cut over the eye. This is them two young sisters what tied themselves together with a handkecher. This the drunken old chap, in a pair of list slippers and a night-cap, wot had offered – it afterwards come out – to make a hole in the water for a quartern of rum stood aforehand, and kept to his word for the first and last time in his life. They pretty well papers the room, you see; but I know 'em all. I'm scholar enough!'

When Esther and Bucket are on the chase for Lady Dedlock in *Bleak House*, the policeman's first call is to the police booth by the Thames, to check its nightly collection of those 'found drowned'. (Once, swimming in the Seine, an appalled Dickens found a corpse floating alongside him – he at first took it for a fellow bather.)

The plunge from the bridge was the favourite mode of ending it, particularly for young pregnant women. It was done at night, lest any public-minded citizen tried to save them. The river on its daily return to the ocean carried what the city no longer wanted or could use. Nothing among it was more poignant than its cargo of nocturnal suicide.

৬ Thames (3. Corruption) ৬

Chapter 3 ('Home') of *Little Dorrit* describes the hero's return from quarantine in Marseilles – a filthy, plague-ridden city. London, Arthur discovers, is filthier: or, more precisely, its river is:

At such a happy time, so propitious to the interests of reli-gion and morality, Mr Arthur Clennam, newly arrived from Marseilles by way of Dover, and by Dover coach the Blue-eyed Maid, sat in the window of a coffee-house on Ludgate Hill …

Fifty thousand lairs surrounded him where people lived so unwholesomely that fair water put into their crowded rooms on Saturday night, would be corrupt on Sunday morning ... Miles of close wells and pits of houses, where the inhabitants gasped for air, stretched far away towards every point of the compass. Through the heart of the town *a deadly sewer ebbed and flowed, in the place of a fine fresh river.* [My italics]

The point being made is that the Thames is a sewer and that its sewage is the food of crime, destitution, death, and moral corruption.

It is not easy to recover a sense of how passionate Victorians like Dickens were about sanitation. But when he addressed the Metropolitan Association in 1854 and said that 'Searching Sanitary Reform must precede all other social remedies', he meant it. Parliament itself could not have been ignorant of how urgent it was when the 'Great Stink' of the abnormally hot summer of 1858 closed Westminster down. The probability is that John Harmon (see above) would not have survived his dunking in the Thames, at least without severe illness.

In London Dickens's 'searching sanitary reform' meant many things: clean water, decent domestic toilets (dry earth, or ceramic and flush), underground sewers and, of course, purifying the Thames that it might, in its daily ebb and flow, purify London.

Incredibly, the Victorians did it. Joseph Bazalgette put sewers under the London streets (they still work for the city) and embanked the river – at least keeping its infections in bounds. John Snow (*see* 'Blue Death') was one of the heroes who purified the city's drinking water.

When Victoria died in 1901, she left the twentieth century a cleaner city, and a cleaner Thames. Dickens did his bit for that.

ல Tics ๛

For Dickens verbal, gestural, and sartorial tics form the very basis
of characterisation. It can be demonstrated in the form of a quiz.

1. Which character repeatedly lifts himself up by his hair?
2. Which character repeatedly forms his mouth into the shape of
    an iron letterbox?
3. Who is the character in Dickens who vociferates 'humbug'?
4. Which Dickens character repeatedly washes his hands?
5. Which Dickens character is neurotic about the East Wind?
6. Which Dickens character describes himself, repeatedly, as 'very
    'umble'?
7. Which character is repeatedly described as 'Cleopatra'?
8. For whom is life 'aw a muddle'?
9. Which is the only Dickens character to use 'My Dear' more
    than five times?
10. Whose jolly ejaculation is 'What Larks!'?

The literary critic will argue that Dickens is an arch metonymist.
He uses the part to identify the whole. Think 'umbrella' and the
whole dowdy person of Mrs Gamp is evoked. George Orwell calls
it 'the typical Dickens detail … He is all fragments, all details –
rotten architecture, but wonderful gargoyles.'

This 'characterisation by characteristic', or 'gargoylism', could
have been a verbal economy forced on him by his deadline-driven
apprenticeship in journalism and his lifetime practice of no less
deadline-driven serialisation, in 'teaspoonful' measures often,
which left no space for anything but signature details.

It could also be more than this. Psychologists have become
interested in Dickens's uncannily accurate descriptions of motor,

phonic, and behavioural tics. Tourette's syndrome was first described by the French neurologist Georges Gilles de la Tourette in the late nineteenth century. It's only relatively recently (mainly through the popular books of Oliver Sacks) that the syndrome has become familiar to the general public. Dickens is a positive treasure of *tourettisme.*

Dickens had, of course, his own tics (*see* 'Bedding'). It is reported that he would comb his hair up to a hundred times a day, sometimes while dining – it did not always charm his fellow diners. It is not, however, recorded that he ever lifted himself up by his hair.

(Answers to the above questionnaire are scarcely necessary: 1. Mr Pocket; 2. Wemmick; 3. Scrooge; 4. Jaggers; 5. Mr Jarndyce; 6. Uriah Heep; 7. Mrs Skewton; 8. Stephen Blackpool; 9. Fagin; 10. Joe Gargery.)

∽ Trains ∾

There are, Humphry House observes in *The Dickens World*, two Dickens worlds: one before and one after the coming of the railway. The first, the world of the stagecoach, is looked back to, nostalgically. The second, the world of modern machines, is looked forward to, fearfully – nowhere more so than in Mr Dombey's ride from Euston Station (newly erected) to Leamington:

Away, with a shriek, and a roar, and a rattle, from the town, burrowing among the dwellings of men and making the streets hum, flashing out into the meadows for a moment, mining in through the damp earth, booming on in darkness and heavy air, bursting out again into the sunny day so bright and wide; away,

with a shriek, and a roar, and a rattle, through the fields, through
the woods, through the corn, through the hay, through the
chalk, through the mould, through the clay, through the rock,
among objects close at hand and almost in the grasp, ever flying
from the traveller, and a deceitful distance ever moving slowly
within him: like as in the track of the remorseless monster,
Death!

Oddly, the railway was almost the death of Dickens. On 9 June
1865 he was coming back from France. His mistress Ellen Ternan
and her mother were in a private first-class carriage with him, and
the manuscript of the latest instalment of *Our Mutual Friend* was
in the pocket of his coat in the rack overhead. Travelling at 50mph,
their train hurtled into an unrepaired viaduct at Staplehurst in
Kent. All the first-class passengers except Dickens and the women
accompanying him fell to their deaths into the river bed below.

Dickens performed heroically in the wreckage, saving lives and
(as an afterthought) his manuscript. But as his daughter Mamie
recalled, his health deteriorated catastrophically after the accident.
His heart began to fail, as did his other ticker. 'It is remarkable that
my watch (a special chronometer)', he wrote, 'has never gone quite
correctly since, and to this day there sometimes comes over me, on
a railway and in a hansom-cab, or any sort of conveyance, for a few
seconds, a vague sense of dread.' Mamie adds:

I have often seen this dread come upon him, and on one occasion, which I especially recall, while we were on our way from
London to our little country station, where the carriage was to
meet us, my father suddenly clutched the arms of the railway
carriage seat, while his face grew ashy pale, and great drops of
perspiration stood upon his forehead, and though he tried hard

to master the dread, it was so strong that he had to leave the train at the next station.

His heart stopped, five years after the accident to the day, on the 9th of June. Whether his 'special chronometer' stopped on that ominous day as well is not recorded.

☙ Warmint ❧

That, of course, is what the convict Magwitch calls himself: 'I am a warmint.' The Artful Dodger, according to the arresting policeman, is an incorrigible 'wagabond'. Tony Weller calls his beloved son 'Samivel Veller'. And, of course, there's nothing that young Sam likes better than a 'weal pie'. Jo the Sweeper's repeated tribute to Captain Nemo is: 'He wos wery good to me, he wos.'

The late eighteenth-century historian of elocution, John Walker, records the v/w transposition as rampant in lower-class London of his time. This particular feature in the cockney dialect has since entirely disappeared. Others (the glottal stop, the shortenin(g) of the present participles, uncertainty about aitches) have survived.

George Orwell, doing his down-and-out stuff, was perplexed by the v/w disappearance, as was George Bernard Shaw when writing *Pygmalion*. Henry Higgins is rock solid on his v's and w's. The transposition was probably on the wane towards the middle of Dickens's lifetime. He is sometimes unfairly accused of inventing something that never existed, although his fiction may well have suggested that what he heard as a lad, in Camden, was still universal decades later among the whole London underclass. Historical linguists are divided on the question.

No one has a convincing argument for the feature's passing. But its widespread presence in Dickens's fiction witnesses to his lifelong authorial struggle to get the rigidly Procrustean 26 letters of the English alphabet to bend to what his ear heard. It's a challenge for the reader as well. How to 'voice' Dickens's fiction? Consider the following ripe example from young Weller in *The Pickwick Papers*, addressing the court and putting on the style, linguistically:

> 'I had a reg'lar new fit out o' clothes that mornin', gen'l'men of the jury,' said Sam, 'and that was a wery partickler and uncommon circumstance vith me in those days. … If they wos a pair o' patent double million magnifyin' gas microscopes of hextra power, p'raps I might be able to see through a flight o' stairs and a deal door; but bein' only eyes, you see, my wision's limited.'

You can read it, you can translate it, you can laugh at it, but can you *hear* it? If so, wery vell done. Wery vell, my son.

∾ Zoo Horrors ∾

Dickens was an animal lover. If one drew up a table of those animals he loved, dogs and ravens would contest the top position; rats, cats and 'serpents' the lowest.

The Zoological Society gardens (a scientific institution) opened to the public in 1847 as the London Zoo – and promptly became one of the capital's principal 'entertainments of the people'. Dickens was not at all entertained – nor did he think his fellow Londoners should have been – by what went on in the 'Snake Room'.

As his friend and biographer John Forster records, he was particularly horrified by witnessing the reptiles' feeding time (interestingly, he could not resist watching it – fascination always combines with horror in Dickens). It was for him even worse than watching a cat 'play' with a bird – something that often crops up as a simile in his writing.

The 'serpents' were fed live birds, rabbits, and guinea-pigs. It gave Dickens waking nightmares of snakes in his study, crawling up the legs of his desk, like the viper in Conan Doyle's 'The Speckled Band'. In the Snake Room he watched, paralysed with terror, as a guinea-pig waited, similarly paralysed, to be consumed. Birds fluttered and hurled themselves against the cage in doomed attempts to escape the remorseless fangs. 'Please to imagine', Dickens told Forster,

> two small serpents, one beginning on the tail of a white mouse, and one on the head, and each pulling his own way, and the mouse very much alive all the time, with the middle of him madly writhing.

Dickens was even more appalled at the public relish for the 'feeding the serpents' spectacle, which rivalled the notorious licentiousness of what went on in the monkey house – from whose sexual naughtiness prudent Victorian parents shielded their offspring.

It's odd that a man who could watch the execution of Courvoisier, or a beheading in Rome relatively calmly (*see* 'Courvoisier' and 'Blade or Rope?'), should have been so touched. One thinks none the worse of him for the soft-heartedness. Or for the RSPCA, founded by equally soft-hearted Victorians, and the Queen herself who granted the royal epithet in 1840.